PRESENT TRUTH IN THE REAL WORLD

Jon Paulien

PRESENT TRUTH IN THE REAL WORLD

The Adventist struggle to keep and share faith in a secular society

Jon Paulien

Pacific Press Publishing Association
Boise, Idaho
Oshawa, Ontario, Canada

Edited by Marvin Moore
Designed by Dennis Ferree
Cover photo by Stan Sinclair
Typeset in 11/13 Century Schoolbook

Printed in United States of America

Unless otherwise mentioned, all Scripture quotations in this book are from the New International Version of the Bible.

Library of Congress Cataloging-in-Publication Data:
Paulien, Jon, 1949-
Present truth in the real world: can Adventists keep and share their faith in a secular society? / Jon Paulien.
p. cm.
Includes bibliographical references.
ISBN 0-8163-1127-7
1. Seventh-day Adventists—Membership. 2. Adventists—Membership. 3. Sabbatarians—Membership. 4. Witness bearing (Christianity). 5. Evangelistic work. I. Title.
BX6154.P33 1993
286.7'32—dc20 92-32316
CIP

93 94 95 96 97 • 5 4 3 2 1

Contents

Dedication

I owe this book to

PAM

My best friend
lover
counselor
and joy
for more than twenty years

Without you
I would live the life of an intellectual idiot
Full of sound and fury
Signifying nothing

Because of you
My life is making a difference
in this world

Thanks
I love you so much

Introduction

The primary purpose of this book lies in its attempt to describe reality. Reality is not always pretty. Reality is not always what we want to hear or know about. But reality is where we all live and move and have our being. Many today have lost confidence in the Seventh-day Adventist Church and its people. But I have found that most Adventists are hungry for truth and hungry for reality. It is the Adventist people, including many God-fearing leaders of this church, who have driven me to publish the ideas that follow in a book. I do not claim to be the last word on the realities our church faces. Many will wish to respond to one point or another. Much brainstorming and experimentation must follow from a reading of this book. I offer it with the prayer that it will precipitate a revival of faithfulness to God's purposes in a new and often bewildering time in Earth's history.

It is not the purpose of this book to offer the "last word" on this subject from Scripture and the Spirit of Prophecy. As a biblical scholar who is also thoroughly immersed in the writings of Ellen White, I usually prefer to approach a subject from the evidence of inspiration. A thorough investigation of these sources, however, would have lengthened the book beyond the endurance of most readers and would probably blunt the compelling force of its glimpse of reality. Guided by my lifelong research in inspiration but without constant reference to it, the content of this book arises out of my observations of the reality that Adventists find themselves in as they seek to live out their faith in a secular world. I am encouraged in this "dangerous" approach by the thousands of Adventists who have heard this material in spoken form and confirmed its observations. I invite readers to search the inspired writings for themselves to see if these things are really so.

A major reality that Adventists face today is that while the church as a whole is growing by leaps and bounds in selected places, we are not experiencing that kind of growth and excitement in most churches in North America. While pastors in New Guinea hardly have time for evangelism because they are so busy screening the thousands that think success in life is spelled "SDA," most pastors in North America, Europe, and Australia are delighted if a handful of people show up for a stop-smoking clinic, much less for spiritual meetings!

The hopelessness and malaise that I sense in so many Anglo churches in North America is to a large degree the result of a process that is called "secularization." *Secularization* means that a society is becoming more and more inclined to view life without reference to God or religion. There is a gradual erosion of belief in the supernatural, a perception that whatever happens is limited to this world and to sense experience. Religious values and practices are increasingly discarded. And the church, as an institution, declines in its influence on the larger society. A secular person or society may not consciously reject religion or God, but God plays a diminishing role in people's day-to-day lives.

In a different category is the word *secularism.* This refers to a consciously adopted philosophy that rejects all forms of religious faith and worship. A secularist may be described as a "missionary" for secularism. He or she is in contrast, however, to the more typical secular person who merely finds religion to be irrelevant to life, but is not hostile toward it.

Many Adventists shy away from outreach to the secular mind-set because they do not believe it is "doable." If someone handed you a basketball for the first time and eight of your first ten shots went in, you would say to yourself, "This isn't difficult at all—I can do this!" But if every shot missed by a mile, you might never touch a ball again.

So it is with witnessing; many Adventists have made ten attempts to reach secular people and missed by a mile every time. This lack of success makes people reluctant even to try.

Another barrier we face in reaching out to the secular mind-set is that Adventists are really much more comfortable in their own cultural setting than they are out in the world. When we are among ourselves, we know how to talk, and we know how to walk. For most Christians, reaching out to secular people is like entering a foreign land. We hear filthy language and dirty jokes. We smell tobacco smoke and alcohol. We are faced with uncomfortable challenges to our faith nearly every moment. Targeting secular people is not an easy choice to make. It isn't a substitute for the more difficult forms of evangelism—it is *the* most difficult form. If this book will encourage even one person to step out in faith and reach out to secular neighbors, friends, and family, it will have been worth the effort.

Evangelistic success creates excitement and builds churches. What excites me about this topic is that, if taken seriously by a local church, it can put that church at the center of its community's life again. Whenever I share this subject in a church, inevitably there are half a dozen secular people there. They are usually the ones who are the most enthusiastic and say, "If this is the kind of religion you Adventists have, count us in!" To succeed, however, we need to know that there are certain approaches that don't work with secular people. If you can come to understand some of the ways that *do* work, your "hits" will increase and your "misses" will decrease. You probably won't begin with an 80 percent success ratio, but it is exciting to build your percentage with God's help.

A number of areas that could profitably have been dealt with in this book are intentionally left out so that the primary focus is not lost on the reader. One major omission is in the area of "apologetics," the task of finding answers to the many objections that secular people have regarding the existence of God, the reliability of the Bible, the problem of evil, and other issues often used to excuse a disinterest in the Christian faith. Such issues deserve considerable treatment in their own right. Apologetics may not be as crucial to the process as one might expect, however. In my experience, secular people don't normally come to faith as a result of intellectual argument but because of an encounter with the living God. And when God has become real to them, their objections usually fall away in light of their new perspective on life.

It should be evident by now that this book is targeted to the issues in a way that particularly concerns Seventh-day Adventist Christians. The basic principles in this book are equally valid for a wider circle of Christians, but the illustrations, examples, and expressions chosen assume that the book will be of primary interest to Seventh-day Adventist readers.

Another omission is the whole area of ministry to our own Adventist youth. Many of our problems in relation to secular outsiders are also problems in relation to the youth who live in our own homes and attend our own churches. Readers attempting to reach youth will find much in this book that will be of use, but little attempt has been made to spell out the relevance of this material to youth ministry. Related to this is the whole issue of attrition in membership. Secularization causes many to leave who once were committed to Christ and the church.

No attempt has been made to relate directly to issues of peace, justice, and societal advancement. Those interested in such issues, however, will note that Part Two does set out a biblical and spiritual rationale for involvement in significant social issues, although the connection is not explicitly made there.

Finally, although this book is very practical in orientation, it aims to set out the big picture rather than a detailed "how-to" approach. However, the general principles concerning how Adventist faith can meet the challenge of a secular world will suggest a variety of creative applications to the reader. Those seeking to develop their understanding further are directed to the annotated bibliography at the end of the book.

Some may question whether the age of secularism has not already come to an end with the fall of Communism in Eastern Europe, the onset of the New Age movement, and the increasing strength of evangelicals in North American politics. While these movements certainly bear watching, secularism remains the dominant intellectual force in the so-called first world and is an increasing influence in the third world. Time will tell if the recent resurgence of religious interest in many parts of the world is a harbinger of both end-time revival and end-time apostasy. But for now, the secular mind-set remains one of the major obstacles to evangelistic outreach.

Acknowledgments

A good book is never the product of a single, isolated person. The one most responsible for whatever is worthwhile in this book is my wife, Pam. For more than twenty years she has not been afraid to insist that intellectual ideas are useless unless they make a difference where real people live. She has insisted that if I want to be a blessing to others, I must first learn how to be a blessing to her and our children, as a preacher, a teacher, a friend, a husband, and a father. The discipline I learned in meeting her rigorous expectations has been my greatest asset in life, short of the incomparable riches that can be found only at the cross.

The disciplines of our life together have been combined with gratitude to God for arranging the miracle that brought us each other more than twenty years ago. And, in spite of my many shortcomings, Pam has never failed to regard me as her hero. In striving to become what she sees in me, I have exceeded my own expectations and those of others.

In addition to Pam, God has given me three men—lifelong friends who have the strength and the courage to tell this intimidating personality the truth, no matter what the cost. Al Coley, Gaspar Colon, and Ed Dickerson have always "been there" when I needed support, and have been direct and effective when I needed to see myself as others see me. Without them, my life and this book would have been much the worse.

In addition to these treasured friends, several individuals contributed directly to this book by taking the time to read an earlier version and provide significant feedback. Kermit Netteburg graced me with fifteen pages of single-spaced type, material so powerful and pertinent that it redirected whole sections of this work. Clifton Davis, Juanita Kretschmar, and Harold Sheffield took time to give meaningful and weighty critique. David Currie, Harold Harker, Doug and Carole Kilcher, and Randy Neall were pivotal in their encouragement.

Marvin Moore, my editor, graced me with his excitement over the manuscript and did the hard work of seeing it through committees, editorial work, and printing to publication. And I must not forget that Fritz Guy and Humberto Rasi convinced the General Conference to sponsor my initial research into this topic more than ten years ago.

I would be remiss not to mention the hundreds of God-fearing Christians, including many Adventists, who took the time to interact with me by mail and/or by word of mouth, sharpening, maturing, and clarifying my ideas from their reading and experience.

Please do not hold any of these people accountable for the obvious weaknesses in this book. But were it not for their input, the book would not have been worth publishing.

Part I

The Challenge of a Secular World

1

God's Style of Communication

Growing up Adventist isn't what it used to be in the sixties. Back then, most Adventists preferred to avoid contact with the world unless such contact took place on Adventist terms. By contrast, in recent years Adventists have held such high-profile positions as governor of Hawaii, deputy assistant to the American secretary of state, head of the Social Security Administration, starting pitcher on a major-league baseball team, Hollywood actor, conductor of a major symphony orchestra, head of state in at least two countries in the third world, and head of an anti-Communist guerilla army. It is a reasonable possibility that by the year 2000, a major country in the South Pacific will be predominantly Seventh-day Adventist. Even now, a sizable percentage of the members of congress and several governors in that country are Adventists. (Recently, in fact, the governor and the opposition party leader in one province were elders in the same church!)

These are exciting and fearful times to be an Adventist. Many of the old rules don't seem to work the way they used to. Many Adventists are trying things we never used to try. The people I've just alluded to know by experience that maintaining a distinctly Adventist faith in a high-profile position is no simple matter. Almost every moment of

2—P.T.R.W.

every day brings the challenge of balancing one's convictions as a Seventh-day Adventist with one's responsibility to the job. It is certainly a big challenge to be a starting pitcher on a major-league team, even if your contract *does* say that you will be given Sabbath off whenever possible!

The challenge of being Adventist in a secular world is not limited to well-known personalities. It involves learning how to get along with neighbors and even relatives—brothers, sisters, parents, children, and grandchildren—who don't look at the world the way you do. Although they might live right next door, Adventism can be as strange and foreign to them as though you've just walked off a spaceship.

The two horizons

But is that really our problem? Shouldn't we just present the message as we know and appreciate it, and if they don't like it, that's just too bad? Life might seem easier that way, but inspiration suggests that the gospel is not heard until it comes to people within their own context. "Lessons must be given to humanity in the language of humanity" (*The Desire of Ages,* 34). People need to be addressed in a language with which they are familiar. The gospel must come to people in context. The reason the Adventist message is going like wildfire in places like New Guinea, the Philippines, Kenya, and parts of the Caribbean is that Adventism as we normally express it is exactly what those people are looking for. But in other places the same message seems to fall flat.

I was sitting on the living-room couch in a split-level home. To my left were three or four stairs going up into the bedroom section of the house. The family three-year-old was trying to push a full-size baby carriage down the stairs. In the carriage was a gigantic stuffed animal of some sort. Halfway down the stairs the carriage tipped over, and the animal fell out, tumbled down, and lay in a heap on the floor. She took care of the carriage, went down the stairs, picked up the toy, and "comforted" it.

I figured it was time for a comment, so I said, "I see you helped him out."

"Oh no," she replied. "He fell out all by himself!"

Now what was happening here? We were speaking the same language—simple basic English—yet we were not communicating at all. And that happens more often than we realize when we're dealing with secular people.

Such miscommunication can be embarrassing in the extreme. A missionary couple went upriver into the interior of New Guinea and attempted to reach the Sawi people—a tribe of tree dwellers who had had no previous contact with the outside world. The couple built a little dwelling in the area between several villages, ministered to the people's medical needs, and tried to understand their language and customs. Many of the Sawis settled around them and seemed to appreciate what they were trying to do.

When they had reached a working knowledge of the language, the husband felt that it was time to attempt a presentation of the gospel. He went to one of the villages and told the story of Jesus. He did it well, and he couldn't understand why the people showed little interest in the story of Jesus. They didn't much care what "the greatest Spirit" had done for some far-off tribe (the Jews) in a faraway land. The biblical message did not seem to apply to them in any way that they could understand until the missionary told how Judas betrayed Jesus. Suddenly he had their full attention. They began to signal understanding and appreciation. It became clear that the hero of the story for them was not Jesus, but Judas!

Did the missionary tell the story wrong? No. The problem was that in the Sawi culture, the highest level of respect was reserved for the person who had the intestinal fortitude to betray his best friend. When the tree people heard the gospel story, they were impressed with a man who could keep close company with a powerful figure like Jesus for three years, sharing His food, traveling with Him, and finally betraying Him all by himself without any of the other disciples ever suspecting! Such treachery exceeded all the best examples they had honored through the years.

How does one present the gospel to people like that? The local culture honored and revered behavior that was directly contrary to the gospel. The missionary's presentation of the gospel had been clear, powerful, and convincing from the couple's perspective, yet the story confirmed the people's own hideous practices. The gospel is not understood unless it comes to people in context. But where in that culture was there any useful analogy to the story of redemption?

Shortly after the couple's attempt to share the gospel, war broke out between two of the tribes they had been working with. The couple did their best to intervene in the conflict but to no avail. Finally, in frustration, they told the people that they would have to leave and go to other tribes who would not betray and kill each other. Because the people did not want to lose the economic benefits that came with the couple's presence (better axes, knives, mirrors, medicine, etc.), they promised to make peace. But how could anyone trust a peace pledge in an environment that glorified treachery?

The treacherous culture did, however, allow for an impressive and effective peace ceremony. Warriors from the two tribes faced each other in a clearing in the forest. A leading man from each tribe, trembling in anguish, selected one of his own treasured baby boys and brought him to the most trusted man on the other side. Both babies and names were exchanged. Each member of the tribe that was willing to make peace came and laid their hands on the baby. Each baby became the "peace child." The tribe loved and guarded their peace child, for as long as that child lived, they knew they were safe from attack by the other tribe. Why? Because the other tribe would be afraid to harm one of their own. And after all, any man who would give his own son to his enemies was a man who could be trusted. As long as the peace child lived, the two tribes would be at peace with one another. Following the peace-child ceremony, all the members of both tribes exchanged gifts and names, so that each person was considered a full member of the other tribe.

The couple observed all that had happened and asked many questions. Here was the redemptive analogy they had been looking for. They presented the gospel once more. This time they told about how there was war between heaven and earth. But God so loved the world that He sent a "peace child." He gave His Son to the human "tribe." He lived among us. And because He died, was raised again, and lives forever, God has declared "peace" with the human race, and every tribe and every nation that is willing to accept that "peace child" into their tribe can be at peace with God too. And, while peace among the Sawi people lasted only as long as the peace child lived, permanent peace was available in Jesus, because He now lives forever. God was now on their side, and He would give them new names to celebrate their new characters. As a result of this and other presentations that appealed effectively to the people in terms of their own cultural context, many of the tree dwellers accepted Christ.[1]

This story is a good example of how communication happens. Every person on this earth has what can be called a "horizon." In a physical sense, the horizon of each person in a room is the four walls and the ceiling, with a bit of a view out the windows. That person's horizon is limited by the room in which he happens to be at the moment. In a valley the horizon is limited by the trees and hills, etc. In flat country one can see farther, but from a mountain peak, the horizon is almost unlimited.

Every human being has another kind of horizon—a horizon of the intellect, the emotions, and experience. Our knowledge and experience tend to be limited by schooling, geography, and family background. When we encounter another human being, it is at the points of common interest and common understanding that we can communicate most effectively. The chief value of education is that it is the intellectual equivalent of climbing a mountain. The more education you receive, the broader your horizon, and the greater your potential for influence on others in this world. You become able to communicate particular thoughts in a variety of forms and expressions. What counts is not the form you choose to use but whether the intended meaning is clearly understood by the hearer.

A major purpose of this book is to broaden the reader's horizon to include an understanding of the horizon or world view of secular people. In dealing with the secular environment, Adventists face a problem similar to that of the couple in New Guinea. In interacting with secularized people, we often encounter worldviews so distinct from ours that there is little or no meaningful interaction. What must take place at such times in order for communication to happen? One of the two individuals seeking to communicate must broaden his or her horizon so as to include the other. Whose responsibility should it be to broaden horizons in a witnessing context? "Lessons must be given to humanity in the language of humanity." This statement suggests to me that some Adventists, at least, need to learn how to speak to secular people. As Emil Brunner has said, "The church nowadays must speak . . . primarily to 'heathen.' "[2]

If that is the case, we need to learn how to talk to heathen!

The role of the Holy Spirit

Many Christians, however, object to the idea that secular people need to be met on their terms. "Isn't it the Holy Spirit's role to bridge the gap between people? Doesn't the Bible say that it isn't by might or by power but 'by My Spirit, says the Lord?' " The Holy Spirit is, of course, essential to all effective outreach work. To attempt to carry out any of the suggestions in this book without the guidance and support of the Spirit would be absolute foolishness. (Part Two will focus in detail on the spiritual component of outreach to secular people.) Not only does the Holy Spirit aid Christians in sharing their faith; He is also quite capable of communicating directly to any human being regardless of background! Romans 1:18-20, however, indicates that although the Spirit's work is universal, it is generally quite limited in content. Scripture and experience suggest that, as a rule, the Holy Spirit does not function as a substitute for human effort (see, for example, Rom. 10:14).

Let's take Scripture as an example. Is the Bible based on golden plates that came down out of heaven? Word for word? No. Scripture was given in the time, place, language, and culture of specific human beings. The knowledge, experience, and background of the biblical writers was respected. Paul, with his "Ph.D.," expressed the revelation he received from God in a different way than did Peter, the fisherman. John wrote in simple, clear, almost childlike Greek. On the other hand, the author of Hebrews has the most complex and literary Greek in all the New Testament with the exception of the first four verses of Luke. In Matthew, you have someone who understood the Jewish mind. He continually showed how the life of Jesus fulfilled the Old Testament Scriptures with which the Jews were familiar (see, for example, Matt. 1:22, 23; 2:5, 6, 15, 17, 18). He used Jewish terms without explanation. Mark, on the other hand, reached out to the Gentile mind. He explained Jewish terms to his non-Jewish audience (compare, for example, Mark 14:12 with Matt. 26:17). The Bible writers constantly kept their audiences in mind. Scripture is an illustration of the fact that God expects us, and is even Himself willing, to reach out to people where they are, to speak their language.

Perhaps even more significant than the unique writing styles of the human authors of Scripture is the fact that God even adjusted the content of the visions He gave in order to more effectively communicate to the inspired prophets. The most striking example is found in the book of Daniel, where visions of similar content were given to two people from completely different backgrounds. To Nebuchadnezzar, the heathen king, God portrayed the future world empires by means of an idol (see Dan. 2)! This Nebuchadnezzar could appreciate, since he saw the nations of the world as bright and shining counterparts of the gods that they worshiped. For Daniel, on the other hand, God portrayed the nations of the world as vicious, ravenous beasts that were hurting his people (see Dan. 7). God spoke to each one in language he could understand and appreciate. God meets people where they are.

It is of interest that, because New Testament Greek is quite different from both the classical Greek of Plato and Aristotle and the Greek spoken today, some scholars of a century ago thought the New Testament was written in some special kind of Greek—perhaps even a "heavenly language." Then someone stumbled across an ancient garbage dump in Egypt. It was filled with the remnants of love letters, bills, receipts, and other products of everyday life in the first century. To the shock of many, these papyrus fragments were written in the same language and style as the books of the New Testament! The New Testament was not written in a heavenly language, nor in the cultured language of the traditional elite, but in the everyday language of everyday people. God meets people where they are! The sacred Word was conditioned by the cultural frailty of human beings.

This is clearly articulated in *Selected Messages*, book 1, pages 19 to 22, (emphasis supplied):

> The writers of the Bible had to express their ideas in human language. It was written by human men. These men were inspired of the Holy Spirit. . . .
>
> The Scriptures were given to men, not in a continuous chain of unbroken utterances, but piece by piece through successive generations, as God in His providence saw *a fitting opportunity* to impress man at sundry times and divers places. . . .
>
> The Bible is written by inspired men, but it is not God's mode of thought and expression. It is that of humanity. God, as a writer, is not represented. . . .
>
> The Bible, perfect as it is in its simplicity, does not answer to the great ideas of God; for infinite ideas cannot be perfectly embodied in finite vehicles of thought.

There is an even greater example of how God chooses to meet people where they are. When God Himself came to earth in human flesh, He did not appear as a twentieth-century African or a medieval Frenchman. He came as a first-century Jew living in Palestine, who talked in terms appropriate to the local language and culture, who got dirty, hungry, and tired, and who even at times became frustrated, angry, and sad (see Mark 1:40, 41; 3:4, 5; 6:6; 10:13, 14). God didn't choose to send us a Superstar, but one just like ourselves. The incarnation of Jesus demonstrates the depth of God's commitment to meeting human beings where they are in their specific time, place, language, and circumstances.

It is this incarnational principle that motivated Paul in his missionary endeavors. Paul's clearest reflection on the matter—1 Corinthians 9:19-23—is also a mandate for secular ministry. Paul tells us that it requires considerable sacrifice to reach out to people who are different. The main reason we have little success with secular people is that we haven't chosen to make that sacrifice.

> Though I am free and belong to no man, I make myself a slave to everyone, to win as many as possible. To the Jews I became like a Jew, to win the Jews. To those under the law I became like one under the law (though I myself am not under the law), so as to win those under the law. To those not having the law I became like one not having the law (though I am not free from God's law but am under Christ's law), so as to win those not having the law. To the weak I became weak, to win the weak. I have become all things to all men so that by all possible means I might save some. I do all this for the sake of the gospel, that I may share in its blessings (NIV).

Paul in this passage gives a mandate for secular ministry, for reaching out to other horizons, for learning how to speak to people where they are. And the bonus is that if we are willing to make the necessary sacrifices, there is an excellent chance that many more people will come to Christ than would otherwise do so!

If God is so concerned to meet people where they are, why did Jesus seem to deliberately confuse people in the giving of His parables? (see Mark 4:11, 12). The answer is that Jesus spoke in parables because of the resistance of the people to His message. The parables were a means of bypassing their defense mechanisms in order to introduce a seed of truth. In later life, when circumstances altered their resistance, they might remember Jesus' parables and grasp their significance. Thus, it was never Jesus' ultimate purpose to be obscure, but to get through to some people without bringing His whole mission into jeopardy.

To "finish the work"

There is, perhaps, an even greater reason to learn how to reach secular people than that the Scriptures compel us to. It may also be the key to fulfilling the promise that the gospel would go to the whole world before Jesus returns (sometimes described by Adventists as "finishing the work"). In the book *The Desire of Ages* is a chapter entitled, "The Fullness of the Time." In that chapter Ellen White explains that God spent hundreds of years preparing the world for the coming of Jesus. He was working in the Greek world, in the Roman world, and in the Jewish world, preparing people's minds philosophically for Christ's arrival.

This description fits what we know about history. In all of known human history, the era of the most radical religious change occurred in the first millennium B.C. During this period, people in general moved from devotion to what we would call heathen religions (where religion was associated with the land and the forces of nature) to the philosophical or world religions we are familiar with today. All the great religions of today either had their origin between 800 and 200 B.C. (Judaism, Zoroastrianism, Hinduism, Buddhism, Jainism, Confucianism, Taoism) or are directly dependent on those that did (Christianity, Islam, Sikhism). These religions displaced the primal religions in all but isolated spots.

Ellen White well describes the restlessness that accompanied this great shift in human relation to God: "At this [Christ's] time the systems of heathenism were losing their hold upon the people. Men were weary of pageant and fable. They longed for a religion that could satisfy the heart" (*The Desire of Ages*, 32). Ellen White was so impressed with the importance of this great shift in human religion that she asserted that some of these great "pagan" religionists and philosophers had received the "spirit of inspiration" from God! (see *The Desire of Ages*, 33).

Hellenization—the process by which Greek culture spread around the Mediterranean—prepared the way for Jesus by creating a world in which there was one basic language (Greek) and one overriding culture (Hellenism). In such a context the gospel could spread like wildfire.

Those who study religion today are finding in the current secularization process an almost exact counterpart to the Hellenization that Ellen White said prepared the ancient world for Christ's first coming. If secularization is the modern counterpart of Hellenization, could secularization be God's instrument to prepare the modern world for Christ's second coming?

We are told to expect that before Jesus comes, the gospel will be preached to all nations (see Matt. 24:14; Mark 13:10). It would certainly aid that process if all nations were influenced by one basic language and culture. And it's happening. There *is* one major language in the world today—English. There *is* one increasingly dominant culture—the secular culture originating in the nations of the so-called first world. Secular culture is sweeping the world through the visual and print media. One of the few countries that has resisted the secular tide fairly successfully is Iran. And there are already signs that Iran's resistance may not last long.

I shared some of these things with a student from

Africa. His response was, "This is of no interest to me. It's irrelevant to my situation. That's a Western problem."

About six months after he got back to Africa, I received a letter from him. (It was one of those letters that I put in a special file that I label "Personal Encouragement." I put into that file the letters I want to read over and over again when I'm feeling down.) He said, "When I got back to my country they made me pastor of the church in the capital city because of my master's degree. I have twenty-six Ph.D.s in my church, and everything you talked about is happening right here. Thank God for Andrews University!"

The secularization process that has taken two hundred years in the developed part of the world may take only twenty years in the developing nations. A trip I took to Africa confirmed this fact. With all the influences of Western media (TV, magazines, etc.), secularization is sweeping in so quickly that thought leaders hardly have time to blink. Could this be part of God's plan to finish the work rapidly? If so, then the challenge to Adventists is very clear. If we can learn how to reach secular people, we'll soon be able to reach just about anybody.

This topic is of *critical* importance to the Adventist Church today.

---

1. This story was first told in Don Richardson, *Peace Child* (Ventura, Calif.: Regal Books, 1924).

2. Quoted in Donald Bloesch, *The Christian Witness in a Secular Age* (Minneapolis: Augsburg, 1986), 45.

2

An Adventist Problem

Given all that we discussed in the first chapter, we can still legitimately ask the question, "Do Adventists need to study this topic?" Surely a church that is growing as rapidly as the Seventh-day Adventist Church doesn't need an overhaul of its evangelistic methods!

This is the point at which reality can become quite painful. I want to make it clear, therefore, that I write this book as a committed member of the Seventh-day Adventist Church. I love this church—and not just because I work for it. It is my life. It has brought Christ to me. Nothing in this chapter is intended to tear down or discourage. But we must also live in reality. And the reality is that, although Harvest 90 was tremendously successful in many places (there were a total of two and a half million baptisms around the world between 1985 and 1990), it is not the whole story. And we need to hear the whole story.

Reaching the world with the gospel involves two approaches. One of these is growing the church—increasing the number of members. Bringing the gospel to the world is a sizable task. It requires an "army" of considerable size. Growing the church as rapidly as possible helps to build such an army. We have been quite successful at growing the church. Our membership is now more than seven million around the world. But we have been far less successful at the other approach: reaching the unreached, effectively attracting those who have never heard the gospel. The very strategies that may help to grow the church may cause us to neglect people groups that are resistant to the gospel because they seem to require much effort with little evident result.

In the area of reaching the unreached we're having, at best, limited success. Adventist work is growing rapidly in *parts* of the less-developed world and in certain immigrant subcultures in North America. But in most places we are making very little impact on the vast majority of people. While Adventist work is exploding in countries like New Guinea, the Philippines, and Jamaica, there are also thirty-one countries like Mauritania, Saudi Arabia, and Afghanistan where there are few Adventists, if any, and no organized body of believers. There are 17,000 distinct groups of people who have never heard the story of salvation, who have no Bible, no church, and no Christians witnessing among them. There are 2,300 groups of more than a million people each that do not have a single Adventist among them, much less an active congregation. While Global Mission is beginning to focus our attention on this reality, the work has only begun.

Although the United States is nominally a Christian nation, Adventist work is growing in only a few population segments. For example, during one year that I pastored in New York City, I held meetings three to four nights a week for virtually the whole year. I was targeting white males in particular and was thrilled to baptize twelve with God's help. Then I got on the phone with a friend who was a pastor in a neighboring church in the Northeastern Conference, which specializes in ministry to African-Americans. I had helped him that summer with a three-week tent effort that resulted in the baptism of eighty-three people. When he found out that I worked all year to baptize just twelve, he jokingly said, "What's wrong with you?"

Was something wrong with me? Perhaps not. After all, I had helped him with his tent effort as well. I began to share with him how groups of people are not equally receptive to the gospel.

Suddenly, it became really quiet at the other end of the line. He said, "I just realized something."

"What's that?" I said.

He replied, "I just realized that we baptized eighty-three people, and not a single one is an American."

"You may not be aware of it," I said, "but you're beginning to face the same problems in your community. It's just easier to ignore the problem as long as you still have some receptive groups joining the church."

It doesn't matter whether a person is black, Hispanic, or Asian, after a generation or two in a large American city, a decent income, and a nice home in the suburbs, he or she is as impervious to the gospel as any white person in North America. This is underlined by the results of a study of Hispanic evangelism in southern California. The Hispanic element of the church there doubled every three to four years through the seventies. The study sought to discover what methods might be of general application. Instead, it was discovered that over a twenty-year period, not a single third- or fourth-generation Hispanic was baptized unless he or she was already married to an Adventist or had some other connection with the church. The church was baptizing only immigrants and the children of immigrants. It is, therefore, clear that even in some of the most receptive sectors of society, our impact is surprisingly limited.

That impact is, of course, even more limited in other sectors. A recent evangelistic innovation that has garnered some success is Revelation Seminars. A massive attempt was made, therefore, to reach large numbers of people in a suburb of a major city. The suburb had a population of 60,000 and an average income of $100,000 a year. It was a prototype "yuppie" neighborhood. A hundred thousand dollars was spent on advertising, and forty pastors were brought in to hold Revelation Seminars on nearly every block!

The result? Eight people showed up the first night!

Contact was made with the marketing department at Andrews University in an attempt to figure out what went wrong. With help from the Donnelley Marketing Corporation it was discovered that there are forty-seven socioeconomic groups in North America, from the richest of the rich to the poorest of the poor. Everyone belongs to one of those forty-seven groups. Madison Avenue has you pegged! If they can put one of these forty-seven labels on you, they can tell you the kind of car you drive, the kind of toothpaste you use—even the foods you prefer for breakfast. It's uncanny, but they can do it. That's how much we are like sheep. But the most interesting discovery for our purposes was that among those forty-seven socioeconomic groups, only four or five Anglo clusters respond significantly to Revelation Seminars. (Another five to seven minority clusters also respond well.) A survey showed that out of the sixty thousand people in that suburban community, only twelve fit into one of those four or five groups. Eight out of twelve is a tremendous response to advertising!

It is not my intention to criticize traditional methods of evangelism. Most functioned as long as they did because they were very effective. In fact, quite recently a massive effort involving some sixty Revelation Seminars in Seattle, Washington—a highly secular metropolis—drew almost three thousand people. Methods that are working with a particular target audience ought not to be given up in order to concentrate on another target audience. If what you are currently doing is effective, continue with it.

But in North America we are clearly facing a very serious barrier to reaching most segments of our society with the gospel. And that barrier is a problem of horizons. There are people out there who are not responding to the Adventist message the way most Americans used to respond. Our message does not relate to life as they currently experience it. We just don't seem to make sense.

Mistargeting the message

A further reason that Adventists have difficulty reaching secular people is the way we present our message. For example, the centerpoint of many traditional Adventist evangelistic series is the Sabbath-Sunday issue. I have seen the issue discussed as early as the close of the very first week. That strategy has been effective in many places. But what kind of signal does it send to the secular person? "These people are into issues that are totally irrelevant to me." The issue is certainly not irrelevant in the eyes of God or of those who are in Christ. But to secular people there couldn't be a more irrelevant issue than whether Saturday or Sunday is the right day to go to church. They aren't even sure why anyone would go to church at all, so a debate over the right day to go to church sends a signal to the secular community that the meetings are not worthy of their time and attention.

Adventists are also quite interested in what took place in the year 1844. But secular people very much live in the here and now. If you hold meetings on the significance of what happened in 1844, they will consider it quite irrelevant. Again, the issue is not irrelevant in itself, but it certainly is not relevant to where these people are. The message that we're used to giving appeals to an increasingly limited audience.

Lest this appear totally heretical, it is necessary to

remember that at the Minneapolis General Conference in 1888 Ellen White warned Adventists not to be afraid of "present truth." What did she mean by "present truth"? Present truth is that aspect of truth that is particularly relevant at a given time and place. I have written this book because I believe that within the Seventh-day Adventist belief system there is much that is "present truth"—messages that can communicate with power to secular people; messages that can get a whole community excited. We need to better understand what those messages are. (In the first chapter of Part Three I will make some suggestions of areas where Adventist belief is uniquely well positioned to make an impact in the secular world.) But while our message system may contain elements that appeal to secular people, it is not self-evident in most places.

I do not want to be misunderstood. Traditional Adventist evangelism is built on a long tradition, and I certainly do not suggest abandoning it. There are many types of people in the world. In parts of the third world and some immigrant cultures in North America, nineteenth-century themes and approaches are working just fine. They should be continued. But in so doing we need to realize that we are inadvertently targeting certain types of people and ignoring others. Without realizing it, we may be telling secular people that they are not welcome among us, that our message is not relevant to them. Where it is clear that large segments of a population remain unreached, approaches more compatible with the mind-set of the intended audience need to be tried. This book is a plea to supplement traditional methods with new approaches that will welcome those who are not appealed to by the time-honored approaches of past and present.

The medium is the message

A further barrier between us and secular people is the

group-oriented approach of our public meetings. The group approach is very efficient in terms of time and energy and has served us well for many years. But secular people are rarely reached in groups. They are usually reached best in one-to-one settings. This should not surprise us. A study by Gottfried Oosterwal of Lake Union Adventist churches (published in 1976) indicated that 85 to 90 percent of all baptisms come primarily as a result of personal contact with a relative, friend, or pastor. Public meetings, Adventist media, literature, and journals are considered, by those baptized, to play a significant role in less than one out of four cases. Secular people in particular are even less likely to respond to a group-oriented approach. Thus, we cannot expect "It Is Written" or the "Voice of Prophecy" to reach secular people by themselves. Significant impact in the secular world is largely the result of personal effort.

When it comes to spiritual things, secular people tend also to avoid the lecture approach. They prefer to question and explore and ask troubling questions. They will seldom come to you and say, "What does your church believe? Give me a list of beliefs, and I'll sign the line at the bottom." When secular people decide to become Seventh-day Adventists, they prefer to have a part in their conversion. They want to negotiate their way into the faith. They may say, "Well, all right, this is what you're saying, but would it be OK if I express it this way?" Or they may say, "Is it OK if I don't see this item as all that critical to my personal walk with God?" They want to own their faith.

I'll never forget a lovely couple that I baptized in New York City. Just before their scheduled baptism they looked nervous and said, "You know, you've been really great in working with us and stuff, but there's something that really bothers us, and we don't know quite how to tell you."

I said, "Well, what is it? Come on, you can tell me."

They said, "These baptismal vows, we read them and we

believe all these things, but, you gotta understand, all of our relatives are going to be there, and if you read these things just the way they're written, they're going to think we've moved to outer space or something! Do you think you could, maybe, rewrite them a little bit?"

I didn't tell my conference president or my board about this, but the Lord impressed me to go home and do just that. I wrote that the Seventh-day Adventist message is based on two great insights: how to relate to God and how to relate to others. In terms of relating to God, I talked about what Christ had done for us and how, as a result, we gladly serve Him with all of our hearts. If He asks us to worship on Sabbath, we worship on Sabbath. If He asks us to tithe, we tithe. If He asks us to live healthfully, we consider it a fun way to respond to what God has done for us.

I continued by saying that we also respond to Christ's marvelous work for us by living lives of principle in our relations with others. Such principles as modesty, economy, and faithfulness illustrate the self-sacrificing love of Christ to the world. As I shared these refocused vows that Sabbath morning, I kept a close eye on some dear old German ladies who had been church members for sixty years, anticipating the worst. After the service was over, I saw one lady in particular coming straight toward me—just the one I was dreading! As I braced myself, she said to me, "Pastor, I've been in this church sixty years, and I've never heard vows like that before. That's the first time in my whole life that I've really understood why I'm a Seventh-day Adventist!"

I said, "Praise God!" And thanked Him privately also.

Now I'm not suggesting that you should redo the vows for every occasion. And when you do, be careful that you get them right! My point is that when secular people come in, they want to have a part in their conversion. They like to discuss and negotiate, which is a different ballgame than we're accustomed to. Such a process certainly happens more effectively on a one-to-one basis than in a large crowd. Adventists tend to be lecture oriented, but secular people are more responsive when someone takes the time to listen.

Signals we don't mean to send

Another problematic area for reaching people of a secular mind-set is worship. Though it may sound harsh to write it, the typical Seventh-day Adventist worship service invites a secular person *not* to come back. Did you ever bring a neighbor to your church on visitor's day only to wish you hadn't?

Allow me to illustrate the problem. Let us say that you have a nice home in a nice neighborhood, but your neighbors move away and new neighbors move in. They seem to be decent people. Your kids become friends, and as a result you get involved together in some community activities. So you're a bit shocked the day you find out that they're Buddhists.

Some time later your neighbor comes over and says, "You know, you guys are really great neighbors. We've never had neighbors like you. We really appreciate that. My wife and I were thinking that there's something you need to know—something that's really central in our lives—and that is our faith. And we were just wondering, would you be willing to come with us to the Buddhist temple next weekend?"

Of course, being a good Christian you say, "Well, uh, sure . . . sure. We'll be happy to."

But your spouse's reaction later on is, "You promised WHOM? WHAT? NO WAY!"

Let us suppose that your spouse finally agrees to go through with it. What would be going on in your mind as you drove to the temple? No doubt you would express your anxieties to each other. "I wonder what it's going to be like? Do you think they might make us chant? You know, get up and dance around going 'awh-wah-wah'? Wow, that would be embarrassing! I've never chanted before in my whole life. I wouldn't know where to start."

Then your spouse says, "What if they take up a collection and offer it to an idol or something? Should we participate, or should we just act like it's not happening?"

And you add, "What if they have a card at the door to sign, you know, and we get on some kind of Buddhist mailing list? Or a priest comes by Monday night to give us Buddha studies or whatever."

What would your preference be at that moment? To turn around and go home, right? But that would destroy your good relationship with your neighbors, so that is not an option. What is the best you could hope for? Wouldn't it be to go into the temple quietly, sit in a far corner, look around, see what happens, and when the service is over, make a quick and quiet getaway? And hope that nobody noticed you, right? But suppose it doesn't work that way. Right in the middle of the service someone says, "Would all the visitors please stand?" Wouldn't that be embarrassing? There you are in the Buddhist temple, looking like new converts just ripe for the picking, too embarrassed to move.

Can you begin to understand why secular people don't usually feel at home in Adventist churches? What is the first thing we do? As soon as they come in the door, they are expected to sign the guest book or a guest card. One of the big things secular people fear about church is pressure for commitment. They don't want to be cornered into signing something that they might regret later on. They certainly don't want to be embarrassed by being forced to stand up in front of everybody and be the object of attention of a roomful of strangers.

Singing a hymn can also be a real barrier. Imagine everyone around you singing at the top of their voices, and you never even heard of the song. There are few things more embarrassing than being in a group that is united in doing something and you are unable to participate.

Secular people also intensely dislike manipulation. They fear, for example, being "conned" into giving something in the offering plate when they would really prefer not to. Their settled view of churches is, "All they want is my money." Before they know it, the plate is coming by, and they feel that all eyes are on them. Not long ago I asked my wife, an Adventist for almost twenty years, why she always put a dollar from her personal "mad-money" in every offering plate, since it had already been tithed, etc., as part of the family's budget. Her response was that she feared the embarrassment of being seen not placing anything in the plate! If a pastor's wife of long standing is strongly affected by such pressures, how deep an impact the offering ritual must make on those not accustomed to being in church!

If there is one thing above all others that secular people fear in a media-saturated age, it is boredom. Is it realistic to think that a typical Seventh-day Adventist church service would be of much interest to a secular person the first time they walk in? Would it speak to anything of serious concern to them? If the worship services in your church do not hold the attention of your youth, they will bore the secular visitor as well.

The reality is that secular people are almost totally insulated from Christianity. They don't read their Bibles or listen to sermons. They don't read tracts that someone may press into their hands. If they see a bumper sticker that says, "Honk if you love Jesus," they don't feel like praying or repenting. They just say, "There goes another nut with bumper stickers!" They don't watch Christian television unless Jimmy Swaggert is making another spectacular confession. The reality is that secular people—perhaps 70 percent of Americans—are almost totally insulated from everything that we consider normal. When you really get to know them, you realize they are not at home with these things. I am not suggesting that we have to change everything before we start to reach out to secular people. But we must at least realize that the typical Adventist worship service is not attractive to secular people.

Don't take my word for it, though. If you want to know why secular people are not comfortable in most churches, just ask a few unchurched people why they don't go to church. If they feel free to tell you the truth, their answers will usually fall into one or more of the four categories described above.

I occasionally get to preach in a Congregational church. I search through my notebook of more than a hundred sermons on general topics and find that there aren't very many I can preach in that church without a lot of revision. As Adventists we have our own in-house language. We have our own special way of reasoning to a conclusion. Just the thought of ten secular people walking in and sitting down in the church would drive the average Adventist pastor to distraction. What should he say? And how should he go about saying it? Seventh-day Adventists are rightly concerned about finishing the work. But if we are really serious about it, we need to learn how to speak to secular people.

3

Defining the Secular

What does it mean to be a secular person? How do secular people think? At this stage it will be necessary to use a few big words because they express in an accurate, scientific way the sort of understanding shared by the professionals who have studied how secular people relate to life and its basic issues. It is often difficult to find simple words that accurately express serious concepts. The following basic outline was first presented by theologian Langdon Gilkey in his book *Naming the Whirlwind* and was later popularized by Tony Campolo in his book *A Reasonable Faith*.

The first word that describes how secular people think is *contingency*, which means that everything in this world happens by cause and effect within the historical cycle. In other words, no event needs to be explained in terms of supernatural intervention. Everything that happens is the result of some other event within history and experience. For example, if I am a bitter person, it is because of the way my parents raised me. If I am rich, it is because my parents were rich or because I worked hard. Nothing needs to be ascribed to divine intervention. Furthermore, everything we do causes other things to happen without any supernatural input. Another term for this way of thinking would be *naturalism*.

Although we would be slow to admit it, many Adventists function on a daily basis as though God did not make a significant difference in their lives. We may say otherwise theologically, but in practice most decisions are made more on a scientific basis than on what we perceive Scripture to say. The extent of our modern dependence on the scientific method can be seen when we realize that Luther wrote a tract condemning Copernicus's radical view that the sun is the center of the solar system rather than the earth. He felt that the new astronomy was out of harmony with Scripture. Yet in spite of our respect for Luther, I know of no Adventist who would argue as Luther did. Science has clearly opened our eyes to reality in ways Luther did not expect. But the blessings of science have their dark side for faith. When a person's view of truth is in practice limited to the reality of the five senses, God is crowded out of that person's existence.

In practical terms, then, secular people live out their lives within the boundaries of reality as their five senses experience it. But such a limited reality gives no inherent purpose or meaning to life. If God is not available to direct them, people must take charge of their own lives. And this leads to the second major aspect of secular thinking, which is called *autonomy*. Autonomy is based on the Greek words for "a law unto oneself." Autonomous people no longer sense any need for God's direction. They retain for themselves all the rights and privileges in decision making that people once assigned to God. Meaning does not come down from heaven, nor do the answers to their questions or the solutions to their problems. It is up to each person to decide the meaning of life.

Some people may decide, for example, that meaning ultimately resides in how they are remembered after they are gone. This explains some of the interest in the environment these days. If by my action the world is a better place for my children and my grandchildren, then my life has not been lived in vain. (I am certainly not opposed to environmentalism, but ecology can be promoted for secular as well as Christian reasons.) Others may reason that if they find the right kind of job or marry the right kind of person or raise beautiful and well-behaved children, their lives will be filled with meaning. Still others seek meaning in art, music, travel, or literature. In the grand experience of great art or musical composition they feel transported into a higher plane of existence. By contrast, lives that are centered on drugs, crime, or the selfish pursuit of personal pleasure at the expense of other people are considered to be meaningless, wasted lives.

According to secular philosophy, each person must decide what meaning his or her life will have. Since secular people do not look to God or anyone else to determine their destiny, they are forced to become autonomous, a law unto themselves.

Very closely related to autonomy is the concept of *relativity*, our third basic concept. If there is no supernatural, and if human beings decide their own destiny, then meaning, values, and truth depend on the situation. What is right in one situation may be wrong in another. What is right for one person might be wrong for the next person. Morality becomes a social contract. Whatever the group can agree on becomes the basis for judging all behavior within the group. Homosexuality could be wrong for one generation, yet acceptable for the next. Sex between consenting adults is fine as long as no one is overly shackled by guilt as a result of some quaint notion of morality. Society creates its morals, principles, and "truth" on the basis of social and economic needs. If something is useful or enough people practice it, it can be allowed or even encouraged. Relativity denies that there are objective morals and principles that should control the development of society. There are no absolutes. All values are relative, and any moral system is viable only for the group that creates it. Rather than speaking about "truth" or right and wrong, secular people like to talk about whatever is "right for you."

The power that the principle of relativity has over people's minds is illustrated by the decreasing significance of lifestyle standards among Adventists today. Church standards were based on the concept that there is a God who is actively involved in everyday life and who has the right to tell us what to do in even the most personal and intimate areas of our lives. But once a person begins to question, even unconsciously, God's active involvement in human affairs, many personal standards lose their primary reason for existence.

The fourth and final principle is called *temporality*. Temporality is the idea that this life is all there is. To the secular person, the afterlife, though attractive as a concept, is only wishful thinking conjured up by those who cannot face the fears and anxieties related to death and dying. It would be nice to genuinely believe in life after death, they say, but there is no solid scientific evidence for it. Since this life is all that such a person can be sure of, it is advisable in this life to "get all the gusto you can." This concept is strikingly expressed in a recent athletic shoe commercial on television: "Life is short; play hard."

Temporality means that we arrive on this earth, we live for a short time, then we pass on. There is no lasting significance to anything that we do; there are no rewards or punishments after the close of earthly consciousness. If temporality is valid, then ultimately whatever a person chooses to do is all right as long as he or she doesn't hurt anyone.

This is not an isolated way of thinking. I remember speaking to an Adventist pastor who said, "You know, you wonder sometimes if everything is really going to end up the way we say it is. I sure hope so. But ultimately, the only part of ourselves that we can be sure will still be left behind after we're gone is our children." I don't think this pastor was a perverse man, shamelessly living off the godly expectations of others. He was simply being honest at that moment about some of the doubts and fears that assail us all at one time or another. But such questions illustrate the extent to which the secular mind-set affects even those whose lifework is dedicated to the advancement of the biblical approach to life.

While these are the four basic presuppositions by which secular people face the issues of life, the average person on the street rarely thinks about these things and certainly doesn't use these terms to describe them, any more than you do. These principles of thinking have been handed down to our generation as an unconscious legacy that affects the way we face life in America as we approach the twenty-first century. A secular person is certainly not an atheist, someone who has consciously rejected religion in the ultimate sense. He or she may believe in God, yet not be continually conscious of God's involvement in the practical matters of everyday life. Ninety-four percent of Americans may believe in God, but 70 percent don't go to church. In Australia, where 85 percent of the people say they believe in God, 96 percent don't go to church! The secular person is not an atheist. He or she is simply a person for whom religion has become irrelevant at the practical level of everyday experience.

I should probably avoid leaving the impression that all secular people think exactly alike. As will become obvious in Part Three, secular people are as diverse as snowflakes, even though there are some common patterns in the way they think. That diversity, of course, is the inevitable consequence of autonomy and relativity. If each person strives for meaning and determines values for himself or herself, there will be great diversity of belief and lifestyle among secular people.

What kinds of people become secular?

What kind of person is more likely to become secular? What kind is more likely to maintain faith? What characteristics place one under the umbrella of secular influence? All other things being equal, men are more likely to be secular than women. Observe the typical Adventist church located away from one of our institutions. Among the adults, such a church will often consist of two-thirds to three-quarters women. I can think of churches of as many as a hundred members that include only one or two fully committed men. The rest are members because of their families or for some other social reason. Recent research by the Office of Human Relations discovered that women make up more than 75 percent of the entire membership of some conferences. Now I am certainly thankful for every woman who has responded to the call of God. But somehow, in the way we approach people, men are generally being turned off. Targeting males may need to become a conscious priority. Without seeking to neglect the spiritual needs of women in my congregation, throughout my ministry I have sought to make reaching men a priority. As a result, the majority of my baptisms have been men, and usually young men. But at times it required breaking the ministerial mold.

Perhaps a brief example will help. I tried to visit an elderly shut-in member of one of my churches every couple of months, even though she lived with her son fifty miles away. The son had resisted all attempts at his soul for thirty years and was threatening to sue the conference over their handling of his mother's trust account. I was unable to make a dent in his anti-Adventist shell. One day, on a sudden impression, I asked if he liked football. He did. I mentioned that I didn't have a TV and would he enjoy it if

I came some Sunday afternoon and combined a visit to his mother with a football game? He seemed hardly able to contain his enthusiasm.

When the day came, he had ordered snacks and nonalcoholic drinks, and set up a special chair for "his pastor." We enjoyed the game, after which I visited his mother and went home, not realizing what had happened in his mind that day. On my next visit, he asked if I could spend a little time with him after I had visited his mother downstairs. When I came up, he broke down in tears, sharing his fears for the future and especially his fear of where he would end up in the afterlife. Somehow, the man who had driven fifty miles to watch a football game with him could now be trusted with his true feelings. I have rarely felt as honored as I did that day. I wonder how many men I have turned off because I was too busy to share in their "trivial" pursuits.

All other things being equal, young people are more likely to be secular than elderly people. Again, one can verify this proposition by a look at the typical Adventist church outside our educational institutions. All other things being equal, people who live in cities are more likely to be secular than those who live in rural areas. People with more education are more likely to be secular than those with less education.

The rich are far more likely to be secular than the poor. This is partly true, at least, because the rich are in a position to take care of their own needs to a large degree and may not feel a need for God. But wealth also provides access to options and opportunities, such as travel, that expose one to a variety of secular influences.

People who travel a lot—who speak in Australia one week, California the next, and teach in Michigan the rest of the time—are more likely to be secular than those who spend a lifetime in a single locality. Why is this? Because travel, like education, brings one into contact with a variety of people and ideas. To use a simple illustration, in Europe they have latches instead of doorknobs. The reaction of many first-time American visitors to latches is, "Boy, these people are stupid. Don't they know how to make a doorknob?" But after a while they discover that latches are very useful. If their arms are filled with packages, they can open the door with an elbow. Try doing that with a doorknob! After a while they are no longer sure that the American way of opening doors is all that great. Similarly, a wide variety of claims to truth makes it increasingly difficult to hold strong convictions.

For much the same reason, people who are constantly in the public eye are far more likely to be secular than are people who live secluded lives. Hermits do not get exposed to many new ideas! (That is why one of the best ways to maintain faith in a secular world is to schedule periods of "derived seclusion," otherwise known as devotional time, where the spiritual batteries can be recharged for the battle of life. Public people need this even more than most.)

People who work in factories are more likely to be secular than people who work in agriculture. On the other hand, people who work in information industries—bankers, computer programmers, teachers, etc.—are far more likely to be secular than those who work in manufacturing. Unless drastic measures are taken to prevent it, a mobile, public person who works in an information industry is marked for secularization. Note the table on page 51, which summarizes the above discussion.

Most people, obviously, do not fit completely on one side or the other of this profile. There are many godly pastors on the secular side of the profile. On the other hand, many secular people fit the more religious side of the profile to a large degree. The purpose of these comparisons is to identify the kinds of people who are more exposed to secular influences than most. As we become more aware of how secular thinking impacts our lives as Christians, we will be better able to deal with the chalenges of secularization in a constructive way.

Secular	**Religious**
Male	Female
Young	Old
Urban	Rural
More educated	Less educated
Rich	Poor
Mobile	Stationary
Public	Secluded
Industrial	Agricultural
Information	Manufacturing

4

Becoming Secular

Why do males tend to be more secular than females? Why do urban people tend to be more secular than rural people? Why do public people tend to be more secular than people who live secluded lives? Because people on the left side of the last chapter's profile are more exposed to secularizing forces than are those on the right side. What influences in society cause people to become more secular? Three major influences can be identified: scientific reason, pluralism, and privatization.

Science

First, and perhaps foremost, is scientific reason. In today's world most people make decisions and solve problems on the basis of science and the scientific method. They observe a situation. They gather information about it. They talk to other people who have experienced similar situations. They formulate an explanation for what they see and experiment with possible solutions. In the end they put all the information together and make a decision. And whether they know it or not, the process that they went through in making that decision is known as scientific method. The scientific way of reasoning affects everything we do and everything we believe.

This is not the way people solved problems in Bible

times. When Daniel and his three friends faced an information deficit, their first thought was prayer, not research. Instead of getting the "think tank" together and interviewing other wise men for information to help them satisfy the king, they went immediately to their knees.

This is not to put down the tremendous benefits that have come to us as a result of a scientific approach to problems. But because science cannot deal with the supernatural—because it can operate only within the realm of what can be observed with our natural senses—it has a natural bias toward explaining what happens in life as though God either doesn't exist or is uninvolved in the natural processes of life. Furthermore, science has rightly demonstrated that many phenomena once assumed to be the action of God can be explained in natural terms. Therefore, every increase in the credibility of science has lessened the credibility of religion.

Let me illustrate with an analogy drawn from small-town America in the nineteenth-century Midwest. In such an Anglo-German setting, one would expect a Lutheran church on one side of the town square and a Methodist church on the other. Let us imagine the people in town are feuding over which church more accurately reflects the will of God. One night lightning strikes the Methodist church and burns it to the ground. What is everybody in town thinking the next day? "Looks like God put His word in and settled the matter, didn't He?" It was natural back then to explain every event on the basis of God's direct intervention. What do you suppose happened to the faith of those people when they discovered that a little piece of metal placed on top of that Methodist church would have deflected the wrath of God and prevented the church from burning down? Because science often "works" where faith seems to have failed, it makes faith explanations less convincing than they used to be. What was once ascribed to

God can now be explained in terms of natural cause and effect—contingency, if you please. As God is more and more removed from everyday life, people sense the absence of God and increasingly live as though He did not matter.

The main difference between religion and science is the difference between truth and reality. Because they were raised in a scientific world, secular people see no difference between the two. Truth and reality are the same thing. And what is reality? To the secular person, reality is what the five senses can perceive: what we can see, hear, taste, smell, and touch. That is reality. But Christians believe that truth is bigger than sense reality. We believe there are other realities that transcend the five senses. Although we all make use of science every day, there is a fundamental clash between the scientific world view and the Christian one. When a cosmonaut circles the earth and says, "I didn't see God or angels up there," he is denying truth on the basis of perceived reality.

The more people rely on science in their daily lives (and I mean science in the broadest sense—not just the physical sciences, but also the psychological and social sciences), the more difficult it is to maintain a truth that transcends the five senses. That is why scientific reason leads to a decrease of faith in society as a whole. This is not to suggest that Christians need to go back to a prescientific world. That is neither possible nor practical. But we need to recognize the powerful impact on faith that scientific reason has had and continues to have on Western thinking, and increasingly throughout the entire world.

Pluralism

A second major secularizing influence is pluralism. Pluralism means that many religious persuasions are tolerated and no single one of them is dominant. In nineteenth-century America it was much easier to develop and maintain faith than it is today. Nineteenth-century America was a lot like an Adventist camp meeting today, where everyone believes the same things. When you meet someone on the road, you say, "Happy Sabbath," and the other person replies, "Praise the Lord. It's a beautiful day, isn't it?" What happens at that moment? Another human being has affirmed your faith, and your faith becomes stronger as a result. That is why retreats have become so popular. When we are with people who believe as we do, we find our own faith supported and encouraged.

Contrast the camp-meeting experience with what happens to faith in a secular world. The first twelve people you meet may represent thirteen religions or nonreligions. If you were to say, "Happy Sabbath," they would probably reply, "Huh? What is Sabbath?" Constant interaction with conflicting ideas tends to erode faith.

Pluralism explains why higher education often destroys faith. It exposes believers to a wide variety of options for explaining most things in life. The positive side of education is that it broadens one's horizons and makes one better able to reach different classes of people. The pastor who has been to the seminary is able to effectively reach a larger variety of people both inside and outside the church than one who hasn't, all other things being equal. But the downside of education is that constant bombardment with different ideas will inevitably weaken faith unless drastic measures are instituted to maintain it. Education is not evil in itself, but it is certainly a two-edged sword. A pastor friend located near a great secular university told me that unless he gets into the dorms and contacts Adventist students within the first three weeks after they arrive, he can usually do little for them. In just three weeks they have been overwhelmed with a universe of ideas they had never before been exposed to. In three weeks their faith has crumbled and gone.

Pluralism means that society as a whole provides little or no social support for your faith. This lack of support produces religious uncertainty. The more ideas a person is exposed to, the more difficult he finds it to be certain that his favorite idea is the right one. This explains why certain classes of people tend to be more secular than others. Public people are constantly being exposed to other people and their ideas. Mobile people are constantly running into new ways of thinking and doing things. Urban people are constantly rubbing shoulders with all kinds of ideas and expressions. Young people, of course, are more open to new ideas than are the elderly. The more our life experiences expose us to various ideas, the more difficult it is to maintain faith.

It may be that the main function of Christian radio and television is not evangelism but providing spiritual reinforcement for people who otherwise live in a secular environment. There is certainly little evidence that most secular people listen to Christian radio or watch Christian television. But in a pluralistic age, Christian media can provide the "camp-meeting" atmosphere for those who are already religious. People may watch and listen to *reinforce* their views rather than to *learn new ones*.

Privatization

The third major influence that produces secularization is privatization. Privatization means that it is increasingly considered inappropriate to discuss religion in public. Religion is confined more and more to people's private lives and experiences. A familiar saying comes to mind: "There are two things you don't discuss in public—religion and politics." Religion only makes the news when it has become a matter of secular interest: a pastor slept with the wrong person or stole something out of the offering plate. But religion is considered a private matter.

I'll never forget an NBA championship series a few years ago. The Philadelphia 76ers won the series, and the television media rushed to interview their star player, Julius Erving, better known as "Dr. J." As he was still dripping sweat from the game, they asked him, live on national television, "What is the source of your personal strength? What kind of support system enables you to not only be a great athlete, but a gentleman who cares so much about other people?" Without hesitation he responded, "There are two things. First of all is my family. I give great credit to the role my wife has played in my life. But even more important, I have given my life to Jesus Christ as my Lord and Saviour. He is the center of my life and deserves the credit for every good thing I have done both on and off the court."[1]

He went on for some time on this theme, to the obvious discomfort of the interviewer. But the network could do nothing about it! It was live television, and editing was impossible. At that moment Dr. J transgressed the unwritten norms of secular society. He seized his only chance to reach the millions who thought of him as a hero and role model and offered the message that life is not in basketball, but in Jesus Christ. But what he did was socially unacceptable in a secular society. You don't talk about religion in public. And I have not seen a live interview of Julius Erving on television since!

The church no longer dominates society. It is not a major player in the public sphere. Politics, education, and economics serve secular goals rather than religious ones. And this privatization, this moving faith into the closet, is a factor that makes faith seem increasingly irrelevant to everyday life.

Thus we live in an age of "secular drift." No one plans to become secular. It usually happens gradually in one's experience. Scientific reason, pluralism, and privatization quietly take their toll. People continue to "believe" in some sense, but they have no strong convictions and no spiritual outlet in an organized group experience such as a local church.

As a result of these trends, the structures of society provide less and less support for a religious interpretation of life. Religious convictions become unstable and relative, seeming to be merely matters of preference.

One response to secularization—a response that destroys the relevance of the past and hope for the future—is escape into the present. An "eat, drink, and be merry" lifestyle of sports and entertainment becomes religion of the self, which takes the place of church in a person's life.

Another response to secularization is escape into a group that protects itself by separation from the world. Such groups run the gamut from fairly orthodox Christian "self-supporting" groups to dangerous cults that turn normal people into social and religious misfits. Whatever the type, the community becomes a refuge of peace in a messed-up age.

The most typical response to secular drift is to plunge into the world as it is. If this world is all there is, its tasks and problems are sufficient to absorb all one's attention. Prayer and worship seem like escapes—a waste of time that could be put to better use transforming society. Knowledge is obtained by reason and research rather than by revelation. Secular people seek to create their own values and set their own goals, and they look to God for neither support nor judgment.

Secularization in itself is a fairly neutral thing. On the positive side, by fostering education, science, and toleration, secularization has bettered the lives of many, including Christians. Discrediting superstition has made it more difficult for people to hide from their true needs through religious systems that deny reality.

On the negative side, secularization destroys faith in a number of ways. It makes truth seem relative or irrelevant. It crowds out the spiritual aspects of life in the struggle for secular goals. Furthermore, since secularization has removed the church from the center of life in most places, the church often fails to get the attention of the very secular people who are actively seeking spiritual solutions to life's problems.

Is there any way to avoid the forces of secularization without falling into the trap of denying or escaping reality? This is extremely difficult in a media-saturated age. Although secularism is not a denomination, the most persuasive evangelist that ever lived is preaching a secular message. And secular evangelistic meetings have been held in nearly every Seventh-day Adventist home. I am talking about television.

TV is the most powerful agent of secularization in our society. Through the television scientific reasoning, pluralism, and the privatization of religion bombard homes everywhere. Adventists used to teach that it is necessary to move to the country to get away from the evil influences of society. So I moved out of New York City into a little town of three hundred people, seven miles from the next town. But every morning I watched about twenty kids vandalize my yard while waiting for the school bus. Bring television into a country setting, and the kids grow up with all the latest ideas, fashions, drugs, and violence. Television can go anywhere in the world, literally. Drive past a ranch on the Nevada desert, one hundred miles from the nearest village, and you'll almost certainly see a satellite dish that's picking up television transmissions from downtown New York! And it would work just as well at the North or South Pole. Country living is not what it used to be because of the media and related influences.

Television has become the "wild card" that can bypass

aspects of the secular-influence profile charted above. Television can provide, in one's own living room, the mobility, the urban environment, and the powerful exposure to ideas that used to be available only to those on the left side of the profile.

Many people are concerned about sex and violence on television. And these are valid concerns. But there is plenty of sex and violence in the Bible as well. I once translated 2 Samuel 7-21 from Hebrew. It was mind boggling. David's court was saturated with political intrigue, sexual antics, murder, and rape. But there is a major difference between the Bible and TV. The sex and the violence in the Bible illustrate the consequences of opposing God or living contrary to His laws. The real problem with television is that it glorifies life apart from God. When was the last time anybody prayed and got an answer on prime-time television? When did anyone pay tithe to acknowledge God's ownership of their lives? When was witnessing portrayed as a positive and valuable part of a person's life? The major shaper of philosophy in our world today is a little box in people's homes. But it does not portray life as Christians experience life.

The big problem with television is that it saturates our minds with images of lives in which God does not play a part. Problems are not solved by prayer and the study of the Scriptures but by human ingenuity, skill, and luck. I remember turning on the TV in a motel once and seeing a program called "MacGyver." The unarmed hero is being chased through the back country of Montana by eight Arab terrorists armed to the teeth with machine guns, armored vehicles, and rockets. If I were in his shoes, I would pray earnestly, and so would most people, churched or not! That is the one thing MacGyver doesn't need to do, because he has ingenuity, skill, and some luck on his side. With botanical insight he creates explosive and poisonous weapons out of plants and wipes out the whole bunch without sustaining so much as a scratch! Now this may all be innocent fun in a way, but a steady diet of such material sends a subliminal message that a relationship with God is not relevant to life and its problems.

I am not suggesting that all Adventists must remove the television set from their homes. We have not as a church taken such a stand. Neither am I suggesting that there is some great Hollywood conspiracy to pervert our morals. Television simply portrays normal life as its secular creators perceive normal life. But every Christian needs to be aware that whatever gets your attention gets YOU. If you spend more time with the television set than you do in worship and Bible study, you are in great danger of drifting into secular ways of living and thinking. If your profile indicates that you are vulnerable to secularization, you need to ask yourself what kind of impact your entertainment style is having on your faith.

How Adventists become secular

Before we begin to talk about solutions to the problem of secularization, it may be helpful to look specifically at the process by which an Adventist can become secular. As with gaining weight and growing up, secularization does not normally happen overnight. It is usually a lengthy process. Adventists rarely just get up one day and walk out of the church. Most of those who leave *drift* out of the church gradually over a period of time. They may continue to believe the basic teachings of the church, but they become less and less involved in religious matters on a day-to-day basis. For convenience we will call the process by which an Adventist moves from deep commitment to secular detachment "secular drift."

The first step in the process of secular drift occurs in the private prayer life. In its very secrecy, private prayer is the ultimate personal barometer of spiritual commitment. Prayer is the first thing to go, and even pastors are not immune to secular drift. To be candid, I have had pastors' wives tell me, "My husband hasn't prayed in twenty years except in public." While such cases may be extreme, few Adventists do not admit to at least some struggles in this area. Don't think that an uphill battle for a meaningful devotional life is unique to you. It is a consequence of being Adventist in a secular world. The most immediate impact of secularization is felt in the prayer life. How many of us can say that in our private lives, when no one else is looking, we walk as closely with God as our public profession might indicate?

The next area affected is usually the study life, although for some, especially pastors, Bible study can continue for a long time in the absence of prayer. But while Bible study may continue in such cases, it tends to have less and less personal significance. It is simply something one does as a ritual or because it is part of a job description. Meaningful personal study and prayer can become absent from a person's life for years, yet no one else will know, except perhaps a spouse. The pastor may well be the last one to know that an elder's personal walk with God is a thing of the past.

The third step in secular drift occurs when personal standards of behavior begin to erode. This step may be the first that anyone but your spouse will notice. It is virtually impossible to detect that someone else is struggling in the inward spiritual life unless God chooses to reveal it to you. Although He has occasionally done that for me, it is not His normal procedure. Spiritual distress sends up its first public signal when personal standards begin to slip. I realize that standards are a big issue right now in the church, and I do not wish to address the question of which standards are appropriately enforced in a local church and which are not. But as a pastor I have discovered that when a person has believed for a long time that a particular action is wrong and suddenly acts in a contrary manner, it tends to be a red flag that screams out, "I'm in spiritual trouble."

Let me use a controversial issue among us just to make a point. Although the Seventh-day Adventist Church does not enforce any standard against the wearing of wedding rings, many Adventists sincerely believe that a wedding ring is not in harmony with God's will for them personally. I have learned from experience that when a person has believed for years that he or she should not wear a wedding ring and one Sabbath shows up with one, it is often an indication that the individual is in serious spiritual difficulty. This does not suggest that the wearing of a wedding ring is inherently related to spiritual difficulty. The point I am seeking to make is that whenever there is a significant change in personal standards, it can flag the presence of secular drift. Other early warning signs of secularization can include such areas as the way one relates to the tithe, social drinking, and choices in entertainment.

The fourth step tends to be a decrease in church attendance. You wake up one Sabbath and say, "Oh, it's such a beautiful day; let's go to the mountains." Now you may on occasion have a very good reason to skip church. But as part of the process of secular drift, slippage in church attendance becomes a very public indication that the earlier steps in the process have become quite advanced. Slippage in attendance is usually quite gradual. First you miss once a month, then twice a month, and then you start coming only every other month. Finally, church attendance just seems to be more trouble than it is worth. After a while you don't even miss it.

The fifth step in becoming secular is to begin to doubt the Bible itself; to doubt the afterlife, to doubt whether there really is a God. You pick up the Bible, and it's as if a voice in your head is saying, "What are you reading this for? It's just ink on a page. This is a book like any other book." That is secularism. That is the result of the natural influence of our society, which leads us away from God and a believing relationship with His Word.

The sixth and final step in the process of secular drift is an increasing distrust of institutions. This includes a lack of loyalty to religious institutions of any kind—for example, the institutions and authority structures of the Seventh-day Adventist Church. "No one can tell me what to believe. Nobody can tell me what to do." The most interesting thing about this aspect of secularization is that it is often seen most strongly in groups that are sometimes characterized as "right wing"—groups that would be quick to deny that secularism could have any impact on them. In spite of this denial, such groups tend to manifest some of the same consequences of secularization as their more "left-wing" counterparts. Either extreme may signal danger, but "right-wing" Christians are usually either less aware of it or less willing to admit it.

Since I brought the subject up, I might as well say that I believe every church needs two wings to fly—a left wing and a right wing! The point I am attempting to make is that, in their increasing distrust of Adventist institutions, the so-called right-wing Adventist groups betray that they are far from immune to the influence of secularization.

I'll never forget the pastors' conference where I was speaking on this subject, and the president of the conference was sitting to one side of the group. I made the comment, "I'll bet that your president doesn't feel like he gets half the respect from you that he gave to his conference president when he started out in the ministry." It was as if I had pressed a button. He shot up in the air and said, "You listen to this guy! You listen to this guy! He knows what he's talking about! You wouldn't believe what I have to go through. You wouldn't believe the mail that comes across my desk. Hate! Hate! Hate! And often in four-letter words! And from people who pride themselves on their conservatism." He went on like this for about half an hour.

In my experience, what that president said was true. Some of the most conservative people now tolerate truly bizarre behavior in the name of truth. Satan has subtly spun his web of secularism in both "wings" of the church, hampering our ability to fly together and largely preventing a positive influence on the world. We are all affected by secularization regardless of our theological preferences. The scary thing is, the less you are aware of secular drift, the more spiritually dangerous it becomes. Disrespect for religious authority, whether one recognizes it or not, is the natural outgrowth of contingency, autonomy, and relativity, the philosophical products of the secularization process.

Now secular drift does not always take place in the exact order described above. In special circumstances the order may be altered or even reversed. For example, if a person is embittered by some real or perceived action on the part of a church institution, attendance and loyalty may be affected immediately while prayer, study, and standards linger on for a great while, perhaps even a lifetime. On the other hand, a young person newly exposed to a secular university may abandon the entire spiritual life in such a brief time that the various levels of secular drift can hardly be discerned. What I have shared here is the most typical order in which the process occurs, usually over a fairly lengthy period of time.

People often tell me that my description of secularism and secular people sounds a great deal like most Adventists today, not just the so-called backsliders. I have never intended a deliberate comparison. But the more you become acquainted with Bible-believing Christians of other faiths, the more you suspect that Adventists may be more secularized than the average Christian. If so, secularism has wounded us more than once. It has not only made it more difficult for us to communicate with those who are not Adventists in our communities; it has sapped our own faith as well.

In the previous century Adventists saw themselves as a reform movement within the larger Christian church. Most of the people they worked with did not need an emphasis on Christian spirituality. So the early Adventist emphasis was on assembling logical and reasonable arguments that would persuade people intellectually that they needed to pursue their spirituality along different lines than they had previously. In a world full of Christians, this worked out reasonably well for a generation. But by the year 1888 this approach resulted in an entire generation of Adventists who knew the arguments but were losing touch with a personal God. And in spite of the power of the message that was born in Minneapolis in 1888, to this day Adventist distinctives tend to get more emphasis in most circles than does a living relationship with God.

In a secular world an intellectual faith is no longer sufficient to guard against secular drift. Adventists, therefore, are crying out more and more for a living walk with God, for a taste of His presence. A doctrinal construct by itself may not touch the heart. In Part Two I will try to offer some helpful insights on how to activate and personalize our walk with God in a secular world.

We may summarize the first part of the book by noting that the secular world view has hurt Adventists in at least three distinct ways. First, it has made it more difficult for us to communicate what we believe to others. It has hurt our evangelistic impact in the world. Second, it has, as we have noticed, been extremely damaging to individual faith. We ourselves often feel that we are losing our way with God. And third, it has resulted in great frustration to the Adventist organizational structure. Being an administrator in the Adventist Church today is, if you'll forgive the expression, a hellish experience. A president dreams of a finished work, but everything he attempts seems only to make the situation worse. One's best attempts just aren't good enough anymore. And it is secularization that has clipped the church's wings so that it works against itself.

Part Two moves us now into a discussion of the most vital issue facing us as a church—how to maintain faith in a secular world. You cannot share what you do not have. Part Three goes on to discuss how to share faith in a secular world. Because I am neither gifted nor experienced in administration, I hesitate to say a great deal about the administrative consequences of recent developments. Nevertheless, my study and experimentation has raised ideas that may be helpful to those in administration. A section in the Appendix offers some tentative suggestions on how to more effectively administer the church in a secular world.

---

1. These are his words as I recall them from watching the interview.

Part Two

Keeping Faith in a Secular World

5

Not for Everyone

Our awareness of the impact of a secular society on Adventist faith forces us to take a careful look at the issue of how one maintains faith in a secular world. How can Adventists maintain a strong relationship with God when their neighbors, their friends, and even their family are all pursuing lives directed primarily by secular interests? Although there was no such thing as a full-fledged secular environment anywhere on earth in Bible times, the narratives of how several biblical figures responded to radical faith challenges may help us develop an answer to the above question.

Daniel attended the "University of Babylon" and became prime minister in the Babylonian court. The culture and religion of the Babylonian court was not only totally foreign to Daniel, it was also extremely hostile. Ellen White has some fascinating suggestions on how Daniel maintained his faith in that challenging situation (see *Prophets and Kings*, 479-90). A similar situation to Daniel's is that of Joseph in Egypt. The basic circumstances were the same. Joseph stood alone in a foreign court. Ellen White described how Joseph maintained his faith in prison as well as in Pharaoh's court (see *Patriarchs and Prophets*, 213-23). Ellen White cites Enoch as a particularly interesting example of how to respond to challenges to one's faith (see

Patriarchs and Prophets, 84-89). Enoch spent half his time in the mountains and the other half in the valleys and cities. What was he doing in the mountains? He was recharging his spiritual batteries so that he could come out and deal effectively with the everyday world. He repeated this cycle over and over again. We noticed in Part One that people who travel a lot and live public lives are far more likely to be secular than those who live stationary, secluded lives.

Since the life of a hermit is not a viable option for most of us, it becomes necessary for public people to carve out periods of seclusion where they can become recentered on God. Enoch was creating what I like to call "derived seclusion." He was a public person in the valleys; he was standing alone for God in a very godless age. But he found it necessary from time to time to separate himself from that society to restore his spiritual vision. Enoch moved back and forth between two ages. He was able to live in two different horizons at the same time. In his particular case, it was a mountain horizon and a valley horizon. In his double life Enoch becomes a model for secular ministry.

Radical conservatism

At the risk of being misunderstood, I will try to put a label on Enoch's style of ministry. The ideal philosophy of life for those interested in reaching secular people for Christ is what I call "radical conservatism." I realize that the term *radical* may offend some people, but I use it for lack of a better word to describe the kinds of steps inspiration suggests are necessary in order for us to reach out to other cultures. Radical conservatism sounds like an absolute contradiction in terms, doesn't it? Actually the Bible is full of apparent contradictions in which both parts of the equation are true and necessary. For example, Christ is 100 percent human, yet He is also 100 percent divine. In terms of pure logic, that is an impossibility, but it is true because the Bible clearly teaches both sides of the equation. We're saved by faith apart from works, yet we're not saved without works. For centuries logical people have tried to resolve this tension in the Scriptures, but without success. If you concentrate on faith, you may find yourself overlooking some passage on works. If you concentrate on getting your performance together, you may find yourself boasting more in your accomplishment than in what Christ has done for you. Life is filled with constant battles of this kind.

It is certain that such battles will only escalate when you seek to reach out to secular people. The only way that a committed Seventh-day Adventist can effectively function in the secular world is through a lifestyle of radical conservatism. The radical has to do with how we reach out to secular people; the conservatism has to do with how we maintain our faith in the course of that outreach. This part of the book focuses on the conservative part—how to conserve and even build up faith in a secular environment. The next part explores the radical aspect—how to effectively reach people who find your world to be totally incomprehensible.

At this point we need to return to 1 Corinthians 9, because that is the key biblical text for our topic. Paul was an example of a radical conservative. The radical part comes in verses 19 to 23.

> Though I am free and belong to no man, I make myself a slave to everyone, to win as many as possible. To the Jews I became like a Jew, to win the Jews. To those under the law I became like one under the law (though I myself am not under the law), so as to win those under the law. To those not having the law I became like one not having the law (though I am not

> free from God's law but am under Christ's law), so as to win those not having the law. To the weak I became weak, to win the weak. I have become all things to all men so that by all possible means I might save some. I do all this for the sake of the gospel, that I may share in its blessings.

No doubt it was statements like these that got Paul in a lot of trouble from time to time (see, for example, Acts 21:17-21; 2 Cor. 1, 2; 2 Pet. 3:16). And I must admit that the implications of this passage are challenging.

Paul offers in this passage a strategy for winning more souls, for reaching more kinds of people. Why does Paul do it? "For the sake of the gospel," "to win all the more"—as many souls as possible. Any way you look at it, it is a radical strategy. I wish Paul were here so I could ask him in modern terms, "Paul, what did you mean about 'being all things to everybody'? How does a Seventh-day Adventist Christian relate to such a text in the contemporary world?"

As I was discussing this text in class one day, a student raised his hand. His name was Clifton Davis, a converted Hollywood actor whom I grew to appreciate a great deal as a human being. When I acknowledged him, he said, "I just went to visit one of my old friends in California. You have to understand that in much of Hollywood society, drugs function in much the same way that coffee does elsewhere in American society. It sets the context for relationship, it fuels the conversation. So this friend invites me to join him in the back room behind his operation. Like so many times before, he offered me a reefer [marijuana cigarette]. Would Paul have advised me to take it? What does 'all things to everyone' really mean? You have to understand that to refuse an offer like that, given our past relationship, was to set up a serious barrier between us. Would Paul have accepted?" (Clifton didn't.)

My purpose in mentioning this story is to illustrate how following Paul's counsel may sometimes put the Christian in delicate circumstances. Given the spiritual danger that lurks everywhere in the secular world, why would a Christian place himself or herself in even greater danger in an attempt to reach out to others trapped in that secular way of life? Paul's answer is clear: "I do all this for the sake of the gospel" (1 Cor. 9:23). Jesus Christ did not remain in the isolation of His comfortable heavenly neighborhood, waiting for us to rescue ourselves. He came down, became one of us, reached out to us in our own world—a world that was hostile to everything He stood for. He thereby did for us what we could never have done for ourselves. When Paul acts "for the sake of the gospel," he seeks to bring to the lost the great blessings that Christ had brought to him. In light of the great salvation he had already received, he is compelled to go. Thus, in 1 Corinthians 9 he calls on Christians to follow his example of reaching out to the lost in "radical" ways.

I use the term "radical conservatism" because it illustrates well the tension that outreach to secular society creates in the life of a true Christian. On the one hand is the critical need, through faith, devotions, and a consistent Christian lifestyle, to get our own spiritual house in order. A settled focus in that direction often attracts the label "conservative" or "right wing." On the other hand, when we go out to do secular ministry, we will inevitably be facing difficult choices, visiting places, and doing things that might make conservative Christians uncomfortable. It is hard to do that without being labeled "liberal" or "left wing." I illustrate this tension by means of the term "radical conservatism."

It is inevitable that the person seeking to minister to secular people within an Adventist context will be misunderstood. An excellent example is the television ministry called Faith For Today, which produces the Adventist program "Lifestyle Magazine." Faith For Today has great difficulty raising funds from Adventists because the program is aimed, not at the Adventist audience, but at a more secular audience. "Lifestyle Magazine" seeks to approach secular people where they are. In so doing, however, Faith For Today often finds it difficult not to alienate its own financial support base.

The conservative reaction against secular ministry must, however, be taken seriously. The crucial point of this section of the book is that reaching out to people in the secular environment is an activity that can place the Christian at risk. I must level with you on this point, and I intend to level with you throughout this book. *Ministry in a secular context is dangerous to your spiritual health.* Because of this I must make clear at this point that *secular ministry is not for everybody*. Not every Christian should seek to make a major difference for Christ in radical ministry to a secular world. Many Adventists had better stay "in house" for their own soul's sake and leave it at that.

Why bother to write this book, then? Because thousands of Adventists *have* felt the call to make a difference in the secular world, to make a difference among secular friends, neighbors, and family. And because the Bible makes clear that it needs to be done.

Secular ministry can be a very frightening thing. Every day in the secular world Adventists are faced with unpleasant choices. And they are rarely easy choices. I absolutely hate coffee; the few times in my life when I—whether by accident or knowingly—have drunk some coffee, I got a headache almost instantly, and it stayed with me in each case for a long time. So, I don't touch the stuff by choice—any time, anyplace. However, I also realize that coffee has become the fuel of secular relationships. And I know that at times refusing a cup of coffee has created a barrier in a relationship that I was never fully able to overcome. I have met people who are more skilled than I am at declining things so graciously that it doesn't seem to cause any trouble, but even they confess that knowing what to do in such situations is always a challenge. Life is simplest when there is a clear choice between good and evil. But in the secular world we are more often than not faced with choices between two evils or two goods. Such times require tough and courageous decisions.

A rather scary biblical example of choosing between evils is the story of Esther. Please do not confuse Esther with Daniel. The circumstances were similar, but their responses were quite different. While I can understand that you sometimes have to alter biblical stories a little to protect the innocent, I am a little disappointed that I had to read the book of Esther in the Hebrew before I realized that she didn't become queen as the result of a beauty contest. The Hebrew clearly says that on her contest date she left the house of the virgins to see the king. The next morning, instead of going back to the house of the virgins, she went to the house of the concubines. Do you follow what was going on there? Esther earned the queenship by a one-night stand with the king—she was better than anybody else in bed. She was probably beautiful also, but the king could have determined that without spending the night with her.

Did she maintain all the standards of the "church" while living as the queen? Definitely not. How do we know? Mordecai had commanded her not to reveal her faith to anyone in the court. And the king was surprised to learn many years later that she was a Jew. You could not practice the Jewish lifestyle in the court of Persia without being known any more than Daniel could. You would eat differently, as Daniel did. You would live differently. You would keep the Sabbath. Esther wasn't keeping the Sabbath; she wasn't eating the way Jews ate. In a practical sense she had given up the faith. But perhaps the most troubling thing about it is that there is not a word in the book of Esther that condemns her for doing so. Instead, because she made the choices she did, Esther was in the right place at the right time.

Now I am certainly not writing this book in order to tell everyone to go out and do what Esther did! The point is that God sometimes has agendas that we don't fully understand. Many Adventists have been very critical of Clifton Davis for returning to Hollywood and exposing himself to the dangers there. But when I see the example of Esther, I have to confess that God is *always* bigger than we are and more tolerant than we are. And God can sometimes use methods that we couldn't use to reach people that we couldn't reach.

I find all this most challenging in my own experience. I am a very conservative Adventist by nature—I don't even let my daughters play with Barbie dolls, even though all their friends do. That's conservative, wouldn't you say? There are reasons. Research indicates that an obsession with Barbie dolls in childhood is probably tied in with low self-esteem in teenage girls. After all, nobody is anatomically constructed quite like Barbie. Kids growing up with Barbie as an ideal have trouble being satisfied with the "imperfections" of their own bodies. And that can create other problems in later life. I believe that everyone God made is beautiful in at least some way. I protest at anything that makes us rebel against the way God made us.

I'm a conservative person. My family does not have a television in the house; we haven't had one for the nearly twenty years my wife and I have been married. I am going to such ridiculous lengths to make this point because I don't want to be understood as destroying the foundations of Adventism. That is the opposite of what I intend. But we

Adventists need to broaden our vision. We need to understand that God is BIGGER than our narrow horizon; that God can use people and methods that we would not even dream of at times. In 1 Corinthians 9 Paul is outlining something very, very radical. We must be extremely careful how we implement his counsel. But Part Three of this book offers some tested ideas on how to do it within an Adventist context and with the result of reaching greater numbers of people.

The purpose of this part of the book, however, is not to understand the radical part of Paul's counsel but to get at the kinds of conservative attitudes and practices that are mandatory to the success of secular outreach. It is spiritually dangerous to read 1 Corinthians 9:19-23 out of context. In verses 24 to 27 Paul makes it crystal clear that secular ministry is as dangerous to spirituality as anything gets:

> Do you not know that in a race all the runners run, but only one gets the prize? Run in such a way as to get the prize. Everyone who competes in the games goes into strict training. They do it to get a crown that will not last; but we do it to get a crown that will last forever.

The perishable crown Paul was talking about was the laurel wreath that was placed over the heads of the winners at the Olympics—the ancient version of a gold medal. "All these athletes," Paul said, "are knocking themselves silly for a gold medal. That is all they will get. But the Christian is striving for a medal that will never tarnish—a medal that will last for eternity." What is Paul's point? If athletes can exercise such self-control for a gold medal, what should we, who are looking for an eternal crown, be doing to make sure of our own salvation? So alongside the radical, Paul places the conservative. You cannot separate the two, or secular ministry will not work.

Paul pressed the point home in verses 26, 27:

> Therefore I do not run like a man running aimlessly; I do not fight like a man beating the air. No, I beat my body and make it my slave so that after I have preached to others, I myself will not be disqualified for the prize.

Paul must have enjoyed sports, for they often illustrated his points. In this case he was running and boxing, but he wasn't just shadowboxing or running in circles. It all had a purpose. In his outreach to the world of his day, Paul became "all things to everybody"—a very radical concept. He realized, however, that it was a *dangerous* thing to do. He realized that evangelism is a two-way street. You not only share, but you also learn. When you are dealing with secular people, there is a lot of give and take, and you will be changed by it. Though you may never drink a cup of coffee, you will still be changed by continual encounters with secular people for evangelistic purposes. Paul recognized that and said it was *essential* that those who go out to minister in this way see to their own house, their own body, and their own soul. They need to go into rigorous training, much as Olympic athletes do.

Two models of ministry

Because of the dangers in secular ministry, it is not surprising that the Bible describes two major models of ministry. Secular ministry is not for everyone. There are many people whose souls are at too great a risk to try it. If you are one of those people, read what I have written here, try to understand what's going on, but do not feel obligated to go out and do exactly what Paul did, and certainly not what Esther did!

The two biblical models for ministry can be found in Matthew 5:13-16. Verse 14 uses a figure of speech to describe the model of ministry with which Adventists are most familiar: "You are the light of the world; a city that is set on a hill cannot be hid." A hilltop city is very visible, it is beautiful, and people are attracted to it: "Let's go visit that place. Let's see what's going on there." The city draws people in; its presence is an attracting factor.

This metaphor of ministry is sometimes called the "fortress model." This is the typical Adventist model of outreach. Just as the lighted cities on the hillsides around the Sea of Galilee functioned as beacons guiding those fishing on the lake at night, so the Adventist Church has functioned as a prophetic beacon to society. A fortress-city has walls around it to protect those who are inside from the dangers outside. Every so often, the inhabitants of such a city may send out the army to conduct a "crusade." They open the gates quickly, rush out to snatch up a few captives, bring them back in through the gate, and slam the door. That is the fortress model of ministry.

While the Seventh-day Adventist Church has, in the past, tended to focus mainly on the fortress model, Jesus offers more than one model of ministry. The other model opens up new dimensions of outreach to those who have felt like round pegs in square holes in some of the more traditional approaches. Notice the text:

> You are the salt of the earth. But if the salt loses its saltiness, how can it be made salty again? It is no longer good for anything, except to be thrown out and trampled by men.

"You are the salt of the earth." What kind of ministry model is this? How does salt do its ministry? It mingles with the food and disappears. It becomes part of the crowd, so to speak. But as a result of that ministry, what happens? The food tastes better. The salt has an effect upon the whole. It is a quiet ministry, an infiltration ministry. But the "salt model" of ministry takes one outside the walls of protection. Matthew 5:13, therefore, underlines the same message as 1 Corinthians 9. If the salt becomes tasteless, it will no longer function as salt. It can no longer accomplish anything by infiltration.

That is what radical conservatism is all about. The radical means being scattered out there, mingling with the people where they are. Adventists are not like that by nature. We prefer the other model of ministry that Jesus talks about in verse 14. There is nothing wrong with the fortress model. It is a valid option, according to Jesus. Both fortress-city and salt models are valid. Both of them are needed. I'd like to suggest that "finishing the work" as outlined by Jesus' great commission (see Matt. 28:18-20) involves two tasks. One of those tasks is growing the church, because it is only as the church grows that it can develop the work force necessary to go out and reach the unreached. The Adventist church has now grown to seven million, larger than the combined military of both the United States and the former Soviet Union. Growing the church has progressed significantly. But the other task that must be done is reaching the unreached. It is not enough simply to grow a big church. The gospel must go to all the world as a witness to all nations (see Matt. 24:14).

What adds complexity to the issue is the fact that the two models of ministry can seem to work against each other at times. An outreach activity that effectively brings in people from certain sectors of society may completely stymie outreach to another sector. Let me illustrate. Church growth theory suggests that it is crucial to get everyone's name and address at the door, make sure you welcome them publicly, then make sure you visit them Sunday night right after their first visit to the church service. That is church growth theory. And it works well, for example, for people who are already Christians. A good growth program will usually attract Christians from other churches to your church. And there is nothing wrong with that. A little competition makes everyone better. But, as we saw previously, these very things that help grow a church can turn off the secular people who might come.

I remember a quiet, sweet lady in New York City who came out month after month to every outreach meeting our church held. Everything that I had been taught suggested that I needed to get into her home as quickly as possible. Something in the way she carried herself, however, signaled to me that this was not a good idea. But after some six to eight months, I developed a serious case of ministerial guilt for not visiting her in her home. It was time to do what I had been taught was right, even though I retained the nagging suspicion that in this case it was not right. I parked my car near the neat duplex where she lived. Although every light was on in the apartment where she lived, there was no answer to my repeated ringing of the bell. She never came to another meeting. I had violated an unwritten code of secular privacy. It was one of God's first signals to me that there was more than one right way to do ministry.

Paul and James are good examples of these two models of ministry. Paul tried to be "all things to all people." James, on the other hand, stayed in Jerusalem and kept the fortress together. He boasted to Paul about the thousands of Jews in Jerusalem who were observing the law instead of doing all the radical things that Paul seemed to advocate. "You know, Paul, people around here are wondering if you're still a Christian. What are you going to do to put a stop to these rumors about you?" (see Acts 21:17-25).

It is seriously inaccurate to suggest that life in the early church was paradise compared to today. As I told my wife after our first and only visit to Hawaii recently, "One thing is for sure, there's no place on earth called Paradise." Hawaii is a beautiful place, but no place could live up to the incredible expectations that people have when they go there. It gets cold there occasionally, and the surf isn't always great. And sometimes the fish bite you (at least it happened to me), and you get scraped by the coral under the sea. There is no place on earth called Paradise! In my opinion, Paradise is being wherever God wants you to be and making the most of it.

So it was with the early church. Paul and James had real disagreements. If one reads Acts 21 carefully in the original language, it becomes clear that when Paul paid his last visit to Jerusalem, he was welcomed gladly by only a handful of people. These were probably the remnants of Stephen's ministry as described in Acts 6. But the vast majority of believers in Jerusalem were hostile to Paul, or at least they were suspicious of his intentions. The New Testament tells of at least two instances when even among the apostles there were tensions. Paul and James decided to shake hands and go their separate ways (see Galatians 2:9), and on another occasion Paul and Barnabas did the same thing (see Acts 15:36-40). "You do ministry your way, and I'll do it my way." It may be that we ought to make similar kinds of agreements today. "You have a 'fortress-style ministry'; the Lord is calling me to a 'salt-style ministry.' I need you to pray for me, and you need me to pray for you; I will encourage you, and you can encourage me."

One can find a similar contrast in ministry styles between Jesus and John the Baptist. John the Baptist lived out in the wilderness. He had nobody to preach to unless they were somehow drawn to him. Jesus, on the other hand, lived, for a while at least, in Capernaum, where He mingled with the people. He also went from city to city, and He met people where they were.

Compare Elijah and Elisha. Elijah was out in the wilderness, eating raven's food and drinking mountain water. Elisha lived in town. He was as comfortable in a king's court as in a farmer's dwelling. While Elisha dressed in ordinary clothes, Elijah dressed in a wild man's outfit. You could say that he had his own unique dress code. It is no coincidence that Adventists often call our mission the delivery of an "Elijah message."

We have a choice. We can say, "God has not called us to secular ministry. We have been called to a John the Baptist/James/Elijah type of ministry." That is one option. It is certainly the option most familiar to Adventists. But if God has truly called us to reach all people everywhere, we cannot ignore the need to broaden our approach. It would not be the first time this has happened in our movement. We started out just ministering to former Adventists. Soon we broadened it to include people who had not heard the Millerite message; then we broadened it to foreign-language speakers in America; and finally J. N. Andrews went over to Europe, and the gospel as we understand it began to go to the world *on our terms*. I wonder if it isn't time for the fifth step—to take the gospel to the world *on its terms*, as the missionary couple in New Guinea did, and as Paul outlined it in 1 Corinthians 9.

A good friend in the General Conference recently called my attention to some Ellen White statements I had never noticed. Until I read this portion of her writings, I had the impression that Ellen White was interested in only one kind of ministry—the fortress style. She so consistently advocated separation from the world, even to a special dress code and so forth, that the following passage absolutely shocked me:

> It would be perfectly safe for our youth to enter the colleges of our land if they were converted every day. . . . Now, shall professed Christians refuse to associate with the unconverted, and seek to have no communication with them? No, they are to be with them, in the world and not of the world, but not to partake of their ways, not to be impressed by them, not to have a heart open to their customs and practices. Their associations are to be for the purpose of drawing others to Christ (*Selected Messages*, bk. 3, 231).

That sounds like secular ministry to me. Several Adventist colleges had already been established at the time this statement was written (1891), but she was not talking about Adventist colleges. She had in mind secular campuses. One could rephrase her statement in contemporary terms: "It would be perfectly safe for our youth to enter the secular colleges of our land if . . ." Four years later she repeated the call:

> Those who have the Spirit of God, who have the truth wrought into their very being, should be encouraged to enter colleges, and live the truth, as Daniel and Paul did (ibid., 233).

Perhaps you can now understand the surprise with which I greeted these statements. Selected Adventist youth should be *encouraged* to enter secular colleges. She elaborated on this further:

> There are those who, after becoming established, rooted and grounded in the truth, should enter these

> institutions of learning as students. They can keep the living principles of the truth, and observe the Sabbath, and yet they will have opportunity to work for the Master by dropping seeds of truth in minds and hearts. Under the influence of the Holy Spirit, these seeds will spring up to bear fruit for the glory of God and will result in the saving of souls (ibid., 234).

I do not want to be misunderstood. I am a strong believer in Adventist education. I teach at one of our Adventist institutions. I think that our schools are the best place for most Adventist young people. There are selected young people, however—those who have their act together as Seventh-day Adventist Christians—whom she suggests ought to be encouraged to infiltrate secular campuses for Christ. Such a secular ministry is certainly not for everyone. But that does not mean that selected ones should not be encouraged to go. Ellen White was keenly aware of this dilemma:

> I scarcely dare present this method of labor; for there is danger that those who have no connection with God will place themselves in these schools, and instead of correcting error and diffusing light, will themselves be led astray (ibid.)

At the risk of repeating myself, let me say it again: Secular ministry may be dangerous to your spiritual health. The last thing I want is for the readers of this book to run out and lose their souls. It is not safe unless the person is spiritually prepared for the ordeal. "There is danger that those who have no connection with God will place themselves in these schools and . . . be led astray."

But shall the danger cause us to reject this method of ministry? Notice how Ellen White's statement continues.

"But this work *must* be done and it *will* be done by those who are led and taught of God." Paul was compelled to do it. Jesus and Elisha were compelled to do it, and many who read this book will be compelled to do it. But before the radical must come the conservative, because if you do not have your act together as a Seventh-day Adventist Christian, your attempts to reach secular people will fail, and you may lose your own way in the process. Effective outreach to the secular world must begin in the privacy of one's own walk with God.

6

Communicating With God

How can we maintain faith in a secular world—a faith that will result in successful outreach to secular-minded people? The place to start is with the devotional life, which provides the derived seclusion from the secular environment that allows our spiritual life to flourish. It involves coming apart from the world every day for some time with the Lord. As we noticed earlier, weakness in the devotional life is the first step on the road of secular drift. It causes one to wonder why the devotional lives of so many Adventists are not more energizing than they are.

We tend to live very noisy lives. Even pastors spend their lives running from one thing to another, from one idea to another, from one situation to another, from one emergency to another. And if it is like that in the pastor's study, usually it is even worse at the conference office. We need desperately to slow down. We need desperately to reflect. We need desperately to take stock. I am contending here that this is our greatest need. If you do not have a living relationship with God, please don't try to reach secular people. If you are as secular as the person you are trying to reach, you are on the same spiritual level. Like cannot elevate like. You cannot help a secular person to find God if you do not know Him for yourself. It may be that in helping someone else to search for God, you might find Him for yourself. So don't turn down opportunities to witness. But never try to develop a radical, secular-style ministry if you do not have a living relationship with God. It will not work.

Those ministers, evangelists, and church members who do win secular people succeed because they have a living relationship with God even when they are not aware of the best methods available. When I was pastoring in New York City in the late seventies and early eighties, I knew of a self-supporting institution called Living Springs. These people may have had little idea of the concepts discussed in this book, but they loved the Lord, and somehow, in their special way, they succeeded in reaching selected secular people whom nobody else was reaching. I once sent a hardened street kid up there to deal with some substance abuse problems, and although he was somewhat critical because they seemed out of touch with life as he knew it, he nevertheless decided to commit himself to Christ and the church because of the spiritual warmth and familial atmosphere of the place. A living walk with God is certainly a basic asset in anyone seeking to reach secular people. Secular ministry *must* begin in the devotional room.

In what follows I would like to offer a number of practical suggestions that have helped me to maintain and develop a living walk with God in the face of the inevitable dangers of secular drift. I came by these suggestions, not primarily from reading books, but from personal experimentation and trial. I offer them, not as a cut-and-dried formula that everyone must follow, but as a smorgasbord of ideas from which the reader can pick and choose what seems appropriate to his or her circumstances.

The study life

It is absolutely essential to Christian experience that the devotional life center on the key issues that affect a person's everyday experience. To be devotionally useful, reading must be relevant to present experience, to things that matter in practical terms. Our study lives need to be centered on things that matter. What are the greatest concerns and needs in your life? To center study on matters of lesser concern would certainly be a mistake. Genealogies and prophecies may be of intense intellectual interest, but generally they do not offer practical guidance for the issues of the household, the workplace, and the neighborhood.

Since a personal knowledge of Jesus Christ is the most relevant of all spiritual concerns, I suggest that your devotional study focus on Jesus. He needs to be the very center of your study life. To illustrate in terms of the writings of Ellen White, I have found it helpful to limit myself devotionally to the books in the Conflict Series (the five books that cover the broad scope of the biblical story, from *Patriarchs and Prophets* to *The Great Controversy*) and to the Jesus books (those that center on the life and teachings of Christ: *Christ's Object Lessons*, *The Ministry of Healing*, *Steps to Christ*, and *Thoughts From the Mount of Blessing*). At one time these books on the life of Christ were all going to be part of *The Desire of Ages*, but it just got too big. So Ellen White divided the material into a book on the life of Christ, a book that focused on His healing ministry, a book on the Sermon on the Mount, a book about the parables of Jesus, and a book that focused on practical living. My personal favorite for devotions is a tossup between *Christ's Object Lessons* and *The Ministry of Healing*. The first hundred pages and the last hundred pages of *The Ministry of Healing* are, in my opinion, the very best that Ellen White ever wrote.

As we focus on Jesus, our devotional life will be energized. The best place to develop a relationship with God is to learn to know Jesus.

The amazing thing to me is that, even in our devotional

life, we have a tendency to set secular goals. For example, when I started out in my devotional life, I would say to myself, "Let's see how many pages I can read in the next hour." In devotional reading, the most important thing is to discern God's voice to you personally, not to finish a certain number of pages or master a certain amount of information. If it takes a whole hour to meditate on one sentence, so be it. The devotional life is not the time and place to rush. Take your time; go no farther or faster than you are able to understand what you've been reading. Allow the reading to sink in—let it impact on the very core of your being.

In the process of devotional study, I have found it helpful to write down the insights that God gives me as part of my devotional experience. The reason for this is that people forget what they don't write down. If you are really into the computer age, it may even work well to have a laptop computer at your side as you work through your devotions. I remember a couple of occasions where my heart was so filled with joy and insight that I grabbed the laptop and spent more than an hour recording insights that I have treasured ever since. The new generation may find laptops a more relevant way to maintain faith than using paper and pencil—a mode that is increasingly foreign to the rest of their lives.

I would not limit devotional note taking, however, to the spiritual insights that result from reading. I have found it extremely meaningful to spend time with what I call a "spiritual diary." Most of us live "unreflective lives." We rarely stop to think, "What am I really doing from day to day? Does it make any real difference in the world?" "Am I sensitive to the Lord's leading? Is my work effective for the Lord?" "How am I raising my children? Was I the kind of father I wanted to be yesterday, or were there some real flaws in the way I dealt with my children?" "What are my most important needs right now? How would God want me to meet them?"

Many of us take very little time to reflect on our lives. But the fact is, if we don't keep score of our lives, we will repeat the same errors over and over again. At times when I have neglected my spiritual diary, I can go three to four weeks and not even be aware that I have been exhibiting a nasty temper around the house. Without regular self-examination, we drift into counterproductive behaviors with the same ease that we drift into secularism. If every day we would take time to reflect on the previous day and say, "Did I give glory to God?" there would be an amazing growth of self-awareness. We would begin to see things in ourselves that everyone who knows us can see, but we are blind to. (Perhaps someone should write a book entitled *All the Things You Ever Wanted to Know About Yourself—but Were Afraid to Ask*.) To write down these things in a diary and to meditate on them is to learn how to see ourselves the way God sees us.

Virtually all the great spiritual giants, like Wesley, Luther, and Ellen White, kept diaries most of their lives, and these documents are filled with little tidbits of how God helped them to understand themselves and the world in which they accomplished work for Him. God may impress us that we didn't handle a particular situation very well the previous day; a letter or word of apology may be in order. Or it may become evident that a child or spouse has not received the kind of attention that he or she needs, and a reorienting of our schedule is in order. Or we may become aware that feelings of bitterness related to home or business are undermining our usefulness as Christians. A spiritual diary is probably the best way to prevent oneself from drifting into unproductive behaviors.

Living as we do in the hurry-up world of the information age, some of us will discover a marvelous side effect to keeping a spiritual diary. When we stop and reflect upon our lives, the workaholic atmosphere we live in day by day will begin to calm down. Although it may take forty-five minutes to an hour, the brain waves slow perceptibly from the usual ten thousand RPMs down to idle.

It really works. Taking the time to reflect on the previous twenty-four hours and on what God is doing in your life can really stop you in your tracks. Of course, you are probably thinking, "Who's got an hour? I certainly don't." I will be the first to admit that I struggle with the issue of time, but there is no spiritual substitute for reading and reflection. These exercises take precious time, but they are worth every minute.

A life of prayer

The prayer life is certainly an area of great difficulty for most Adventists in a secular age. I would like to share some ideas in this area, not as a right way or wrong way to maintain a meaningful prayer life, but as practices that have helped me a great deal. If you have found a better way to commune effectively with God, praise the Lord for it. And by all means share it around. I too will be eager to listen. But if your prayer life is not what you would like it to be—and the general silence that usually sets in when I talk about prayer publicly indicates to me that it is an area of great concern for most Adventists—let me share what has helped me.

The attitude in prayer has varied through the ages. By attitude I mean whether you sit, stand, or kneel; whether your eyes are open or shut; whether you fold your hands or put them behind your back or raise them up in the air. These things have more to do with culture than with God's absolute will. When it comes to prayer, I am a pragmatist—if it works, use it. A careful look at the prayers described in the Bible indicates that there is no one right prayer attitude. God is interested above all else in communicating with us, and whatever aids that process is a blessing.

You may not have the same difficulties in prayer that I do, but I find that when I close my eyes and pray silently, my mind wanders almost instantly. I have no idea what causes it, but the minute I close my eyes and try to pray, my mind is off in all kinds of directions, and fifteen minutes later I realize that I have been in another universe for fifteen minutes. I sometimes totally forget that I am in prayer. If I didn't know that many people have the same problem, I would probably be reluctant to discuss this in a public way. But if you can relate to my problem, I am glad to report that I also have a solution.

The solution for me is to pray with my eyes open! That has made all the difference. And frankly, if you read the Bible carefully, you'll discover that many people prayed with their eyes open. Even Jesus lifted up His eyes to heaven when He prayed (see John 11:41).

If you have difficulty focusing your mind in silent prayer, I suggest that you find a special prayer location and then focus your eyes on a particular spot. It could be the carpet or the pattern in the fabric of a couch—it could even be a picture of Jesus. Whatever it is seems less important than having a focal point. I find that a visual focal point helps me to concentrate my thoughts and direct them to God. If something else works for you, that is fine, but I have found that when I close my eyes, it doesn't work. In a media age, we may all need some help in developing our ability to concentrate.

Another thing that I find very helpful is to write out my prayers. It is amazing what the process of writing does to help concentrate the mind on the reality of being in the act of prayer. Take a notebook and a pencil or a pen, and construct a carefully worded prayer to God. Some computer wizards may again find a notebook computer the most relevant way to do this.

Let me illustrate the importance of the writing process to the way people focus on a task. I have made it a personal policy never to accept a major speaking appointment without a written letter of invitation. I do this because I have found that when I have only a verbal agreement over the phone, all kinds of things go wrong. I can arrive in a place only to discover that the people who invited me had completely forgotten the appointment. But selective memory can be even more embarrassing. On one occasion I was asked to be the speaker for a college graduation overseas. The contact person kept calling and calling and calling. Against my better judgment—because I was going to be there anyway—I accepted the appointment. Despite repeated requests, he never wrote me a letter, never communicated in writing. When I arrived for the graduation ceremony, he discovered that he had not ordered an academic robe for me. Everybody from the president on down was wearing the typical robes, all except the speaker! Why? Because the contact person never thought of it. If he had written me a letter, he would have had to think, "Well, what do we each need to do for this to work out? Can the speaker bring his robe, or do we need to order one for him?"

Shortly after that, a conference official in the United States called me five times over a period of fifteen months, inviting me to speak at a workers' meeting, and I said every time, "Write me a letter." I refused to agree to a date without his taking the time to put it in writing. Finally, Andrews University gave me an excuse to play "hardball" with him. I said, "We have a new policy at the university. You have to write the president and ask him for permission to talk to me." Only then did the letter finally get written. In terms of focusing the mind on the full implications of a task or request, there is no substitute for writing. Many of the spiritual greats throughout the ages have written out their prayers, and it is now possible to read them. Many of the psalms in the Bible are written prayers. Writing forces us to wrestle with what we want to share with God. The most important things in life are worthy of that level of attention.

Whatever the method or the attitude in prayer, it is important that we focus on the things in life that matter most to us. One reason that prayer may seem irrelevant to everyday life is that the crucial elements of everyday life are not brought forward to God while in the attitude of prayer. Discuss with God the very things that the journal has revealed are of utmost concern to you at a given time. Share with Him the events of the previous day. Share your concerns about the implications of those events. If the only prayer you know how to pray is in behalf of the missionaries and literature evangelists all over the world, etc., your prayers may border on the vain repetition that Jesus warned about in Matthew 6.

Prayer at the devotional level needs to touch base with the deepest needs of life. We can tell God the things that we cannot tell our spouse, or even a psychiatrist. What better person to unburden your heart to than Someone who knows all about you already, yet loves you just the same. Psychology has a role to play in helping Christians deal with life's major issues, but psychology *with* prayer is even more effective than prayer or psychology alone.

While you have a pad in front of you to write out your prayer, why not let God answer the prayer? I find it amazing how rarely I give God the opportunity to answer my prayers. So often my prayer life goes something like this, "Dear Lord, I'm busy today, so I'll have to be quick. These are the things that bother me, I hope You know about so-and-so, be with the missionaries and literature evangelists, blah, blah, blah! OK! Gotta run now. Amen!"

It reminds me of my well-known friend, Sam Bacchiocchi,

the world's most lovable Italian. I'll never forget the time that I called him to get a "yes" or "no" answer to a question. He picked up the phone, and I said, "Sam, this is Jon Paulien."

"Oh, I'm so glada you called! I wanna tell you abouta my new book. It's a book about da Sabbath. A wonderful book about da Sabbath. In backa you finda these Sabbath recipes, mama mia, my wife she make a lasagna like-a you wouldn't believe, you gotta have these recipes and give them to alla your friends. . . ." He went on for fifteen minutes like this and then all of a sudden said, "Well, I won't take up any more of your time. Goodbye." Click. I had to dial again and say, "Sam, I have a question for you."

Now, I like Sam—we are friends. And he wouldn't be half as much fun if he tried to change his personality. But I mention this incident to illustrate that we often don't let God get a word in edgeways. Try this sometime. When you have finished praying, stay on your knees. Place the pad in front of you, pick up your pencil, and wait. You have put yourself in tune with God. You have examined your life, and you have grasped a clearer picture of Jesus in your devotions. You have talked to God about the things that matter most. You have asked for His presence with you. You are now in a position to receive. So write down whatever comes to mind. Sometimes the thoughts that come may seem silly. But do not try to evaluate them at once. Treat it as spiritual brainstorming. As a result of this kind of activity, there have been times when God has planned my whole day. Someone will come to mind—"Oh, yeah! I haven't thought about that person in weeks. Maybe I should give him a call—see how he's doing. Or maybe I should drop by and visit." The exciting thing is that when I carry out these impressions, I find that the contact came at just the right moment, just when it was needed. God is willing and eager to guide us day by day.

I believe that this is an element we have lost somewhat as Adventists. We have a relatively intellectual and secular religion. We know about God, we talk about God, we talk about the Bible, but when do we really talk to God and let God talk to us? When do we let God speak to our personal needs? When do we let Him speak to our hearts? When do we let Him guide our lives? I realize that there is potential danger in this. I am well aware that impressions can come from the devil. But I also know that a person who has walked with God for twenty years can gradually learn to know God's voice as opposed to other voices. After all, didn't Jesus indicate that His "sheep" would know and follow His voice (see John 10:4, 5, 14-16, 26, 27)?

The only way to explain the incident in which Abraham was commanded to sacrifice his son Isaac is that God knew Abraham would recognize who was speaking to him. The command was directly contrary to Scripture. If Abraham had been an Adventist, he would have ignored the voice because it spoke contrary to Scripture. But Abraham wasn't an Adventist, so he went ahead anyway. Why? Because he knew it was God's voice. How did he know? Because he had been talking to Him for years. Gradually he learned to distinguish God's voice from other voices and from the voices of his own natural desires.

This is the kind of relationship God wants to have with each of us—a living, active relationship. It is also the kind of relationship that will move a secular person out of his or her world. One reason why Adventists seem less effective at reaching secular people than many other Christians is that we have become secularized ourselves. As a result, we have a hard time elevating secular people to an experience that we ourselves do not have. People will not sacrifice the trappings of secular existence for anything less than a living faith that is clearly superior to what they already have.

The great tragedy of Adventism is that not only are we secular ourselves, but we are enmeshed in a religious language and culture that is totally foreign to secular people. We are secular, yet we have great difficulty communicating with secular people. What a tragedy! Lost in both worlds! Missing in action on both counts. And more and more of us are saying that it just is not worth the trouble anymore. The fact that many of our best and brightest no longer see anything worth clinging to in Adventism compels me to appeal that it is not too late. We can learn how to get our own spiritual house in order. And then we can learn how to communicate with secular people. As we do both and in the proper order, we will reclaim many who have dropped out, along with many others who will find a spiritual home for the first time.

There is one final aspect to prayer that I would like to emphasize. In a busy and depressing world, I often need to take time for some "thank therapy." There are times when the only way I can maintain a positive attitude is to spend some intentional and planned time every day thanking the Lord for what He's done for me. I learned this from the ministry of Glenn Coon. He suggested, "Take some time every morning to write down ten things that you're thankful for." The goal is to pray through this list from time to time throughout the day as needed. He underlined the importance of making this exercise as practical as possible. "Thank You, Lord, for the color of the carpet; thank You, Lord, for Ponderosa pines [my candidate for the most beautiful tree in the universe]; thank You, Lord, for the raccoon that went by my window yesterday; thank You, Lord, for the air." Did you ever thank God for air? Where would you be without it? If God ever quit on the job and didn't stock up the air supply, where would you be? And if you feel so depressed that you can't come up with ten things to be thankful for, I have a solution for you: get out a dictionary—it's loaded with gifts of God. Just open any page, and you will find them: apes, apples, apricots, and so on. When was the last time you thanked the Lord for those things?

Yes, I know, this sounds like the most childish thing you ever heard. But I want you to know something—it works. The Bible says, "The joy of the Lord is your strength" (Neh. 8:10). The best way to find the joy of the Lord is through a spirit of gratitude and praise. One of the greatest chapters in all of Ellen White's writings, in my opinion, is the one called "Mind Cure" in *The Ministry of Healing* (pp. 241-259). The basic thrust of that chapter is that a spirit of gratitude and praise is the key to curing the mind of its ills.

We are all sick in some aspect of our mental and emotional experience. We are just beginning to learn about addictions and co-dependency. For instance, if you grew up with an alcoholic or an abusive parent, you will tend to have problems that are related to alcoholism. You may not drink and you may not smoke, but do you exercise your addictive tendencies in a way that is more socially acceptable? Is it OK to become a workaholic or a football-holic or even a sugar-holic? Some even exercise addictive tendencies in their church relationships. I have known many emotionally unhealthy churches. We are all sick to some degree as a result of the sin problem, but to recognize our condition is the first step on the road to recovery. One of the most effective pathways to recovery is to thank God every day for the many benefits He showers on our lives. "Thank You, Lord, for the air that we're breathing. Thank You, Lord, for that carpet—the floor would be quite uncomfortable without it." It is at this practical level that the secular person can see in Christian experience something that is worth making major life changes for.

A strong devotional life, then, serves two purposes for

the Christian struggling to cope with the issues related to life in the secular world. It serves to maintain and strengthen the basic faith relationship with God, and it provides an attractive way of life that can stimulate in secular people an interest in spiritual things. The great interest in the bizarre aberrations of the New Age demonstrates the tremendous hunger secular people have for a living relationship with God.

Facing problems

How can we find time for devotions in the midst of the crushing load of responsibility most of us bear? This is a question I have certainly faced on a repeated basis throughout my Christian experience. Few people have the time to accomplish all that they expect to accomplish in a day. Ultimately it is up to us to decide what is truly worth our time and what is not.

What has helped me more than any other concept of time management is the concept of the "news-hole" mentioned by John Naisbitt in the original book *Megatrends*. He describes how American military intelligence learned more about German capabilities and intentions during World War II by acquiring local newspapers in Germany than by any other means. The reason for this is that local newspapers are priority- and interest-driven. Each paper has a "news-hole" or space devoted to news that is of a fixed size for each issue. Articles are prioritized in two ways. The most important article is top front on the first page; the least important is buried somewhere near the back. Paragraphs within each article are also prioritized in order of importance, the last paragraph being the least crucial to the story. If a new story comes in at the last minute and is of top priority, the news hole is not expanded. Instead, all articles are bumped down in location, and space is created either by dropping the least important article, by cutting the bottom paragraphs out of several articles, or by some combination of the above. The news hole never expands; therefore, whatever is found in the local paper is considered of top priority in interest and importance to the local community.

Our use of time is a lot like that news hole. When new activities clamor for involvement, it is crucial to realize that you can't add anything to life without taking something else away. When I decided to take Ph.D. studies, I realized that I was adding a huge drain on my time. My life would become impossibly complex unless I consciously chose to eliminate some major things from my life. I chose to drop playing the organ and watching spectator sports. I have taken a lot of flak over the former one, but I determined that I could not be an excellent organist and an excellent Bible scholar at the same time I was raising a family. To have tried to do both would have squeezed my family out of my "news hole" by default. I rated my family and my doctoral program as of greater interest and importance than music and sports.

The problem is that most people prefer not to make such choices. They seek to accomplish everything that is set before them (expand the news hole!), and it just does not work. Inevitably, either the family or the devotional life or both are sacrificed on the altar of indecision. Whenever someone asks me to take an office or perform a task these days, I ask myself the question, "What activity will this replace? Is this more important or interesting than what I will have to give up in order to do this?" Life is a choice. If we don't choose, time will choose for us, and we will be unhappy with the choice.

All this has large implications for the devotional part of life. Our time with God is often crowded out by the press of lesser concerns. If we don't choose to spend the best part of every day with God, we will inevitably drift in a secular direction. So the first step in enhancing our devotional experience is to choose to make it a front-page priority in our lives. The danger of secular drift should motivate us to make our time with God the headline event of the day. The great thing about willpower is that it is strengthened by use. Choose to put God first. Say it out loud. Write about it to your friends. Expressing that choice will make the choice stronger.

Another step that has helped me is to make a plan. Decide what in your life needs to go if your devotional experience is to grow. Be careful about adding new assignments or responsibilities. Particularly important are the time and place where devotions occur. Some office workers have found that the only way they can carve out time to spend with the Lord is to go in an hour early to the office. They get there before anybody else gets there, lock the door, put out a sign, "Do Not Disturb," and spend some time with God. For some, the time saved by avoiding rush-hour traffic may be greater than the time spent in devotion!

Whatever time and place you prefer, choose it to minimize the possibility of interruption if at all possible. Early in the morning is the best for most people, particularly if no one else in the family is awake yet. For many families, however, there are no easy solutions. I have a ten-year old, a six-year old, and a four-year old, and when they hear me getting up, they like to come and see what is happening. Some of you can relate to that. A very positive thing that has happened recently is that the ten-year-old has decided to follow my example and spend the first part of every day in "devotions." I am hoping that it is possible to create a family habit, where each member of the family cooperates with the others to create the kind of environment in which devotions can take place.

At times, however, I get up, shower, eat, dress, and get to the office before any secretary, teacher, or student arrives, then lock myself in that office until my time with God is over. Perhaps other options may work for you. Maybe there's a room over your garage where you can be left undisturbed—H. M. S. Richards did that. Whatever your specific solution, it is critical to create a regular time and place. If we don't intentionally create a time and a place, circumstances will see to it that we never get around to devotions. Life is so driven these days that one can even find phones on airplanes. Isn't that disgusting? Right now, it is only possible to call out, and I make sure I don't use it. But when people can start calling you on an airplane, there will be no place to hide anymore!

Every Christian needs a time and a place for seclusion. That includes pastors and conference officials. It is not fair to think that a pastor or conference officer should give you immediate and full attention just because you happened to think of a problem in the last minute. We all need to create space and time to spend with the Lord. And sometimes the only way to do it is to make some hard choices regarding the way we deal with people during that time. Such choices won't make you popular; they may even cause others to think of you as cold, unfeeling, or "uppity." "He has no time for the little people anymore." Although the choices are difficult, they are necessary if we wish to avoid the inevitable slide into secular modes of thinking and living.

I realize that planning is easier for some people than for others. If your personality happens to be the type that prefers to hang loose most of the time, you may need to enlist some help along the way. Counsel with a friend or a pastor who has good planning skills. Invite your family and friends to help you arrange your schedule in order to make God first in your life. Consult with those in your job situation about alternative schedules and/or pay arrangements that free up extra time. Invite God to assist you in this process.

Perhaps more helpful than anything else is accountability. Accountability means that you make a covenant with a trusted friend or family member who will help you stick to your plan. Everyone needs a "hard-nosed" friend who is not afraid to look you in the eye and say, "I'm concerned about where your life is going right now." My idea of a hard-nosed friend would be someone who cares too much not to tell the truth; someone who will call you at 7:17 every morning to ask if you did your devotions that morning as planned; someone who isn't afraid to chew you out now and then so that you can achieve in life what matters most to you. Without friends like that, none of us would know when we were slipping. Invite that friend to monitor your devotional life, your time spent watching TV, your use of money, whatever stands in the way of achieving your goals. Accountability provides strength when we have little strength, and focus when we have a hard time getting focused. Some combination of the above ideas has helped me whenever my devotional life slips.

What if you spend significant time each day with God and nothing seems to be happening? Your prayers seem to go no higher than the ceiling? First, know that every Christian has times like that. Don't pretend that things are going well if they are not. Just keep on studying and praying. Adam Clarke, the author of one of the classic Bible commentary sets, went through a two-year dry spell in which his devotional life was absolutely empty. Two years! But he stuck with it. And when he came out at the other end, he was a much richer person for having gone through that struggle. Even Jesus experienced a dry spell in His relationship with God in the Garden of Gethsemane. Yet that was no reflection on the reality of His walk with His Father.

The problem is that when things are going well devotionally, when we feel that we have our act together spiritually, we tend to become judgmental of the spiritual experience of other people. "We have our act together. What's wrong with them?" Sometimes the Lord allows us to struggle so that we have sympathy with the struggles of others. If we are elders in the church, we need to have mercy on the little ones and realize that if it is a struggle for us, it may be ten times more difficult for them. So the Lord will let you have dry experiences now and then. But keep with the program. Your devotional life is the bottom line, whether or not you feel good about it. There will be days when you skip it, days when you sleep in, days when some emergency comes up. These things do happen. But if they happen, get back with the program again the next day and go on.

Having said this, it is still important to place the devotional life within a larger context. Those who have struggled long and hard in the Christian walk are well aware that a spiritual life that is restricted to the devotional room soon grows stale unless worked out in concrete, everyday action. We turn now to the kind of practical, everyday lifestyle that is crucial to faith maintenance and development in a secular age.

7

A Living Walk With God

When it comes to maintaining Christian faith in a secular world, the concept of "derived seclusion" is critical—finding a regular time and place to be with God in the midst of the secular rat race. I am reminded of a bumper sticker I saw not too long ago: "God is not dead. I talked to Him last night." Secularism happens when you drift away from that walk with God, and you begin to believe what your senses tell you instead of what you know in your experience with God. But without concrete and practical faith-action in the life, the devotional experience can easily become confined to a closet, leading to a schizophrenic existence where faith impacts on the life for a short time each day, followed by an essentially secular existence for the rest of one's experience. Doing battle with secular drift calls for more than just the devotional experience, as effective as that may be.

In his book *The Human Puzzle*, David G. Myers confirms what Ellen White taught a hundred years ago: what a person believes may have relatively little impact on how he or she lives. What happens in the devotional life will have little impact on everyday experience, unless it is accompanied by conscious, corresponding action. When people survey conservative Christian churches, including Adventist churches, they discover that the typical, conservative Christian church often has as much adultery, alcohol addiction, drug use, and physical abuse as the nonchurched culture. These problems are just less visible in the church setting. The reality is that few pastors are permitted to see below the surface of what is going on in their own churches. This is particularly true in the Adventist setting, because our high behavioral standards make it socially unacceptable to confess sins such as adultery, alcohol and drug use, and the abuse of children or spouse. In the secular environment, such problems are coming more and more out in the open. But in a relatively closed society like the Adventist Church, people tend not to talk about their problems, especially not to the pastor, who has considerable control over their continued acceptance in the group. Quite often, therefore, belief in Adventist teaching has relatively little impact on how people live.

The significance of this cannot be overstated. In churches where action does not follow from belief, the church's witness is seriously damaged. While pastors and church leaders may not be aware of how little practice may follow from profession in our churches, our secular neighbors are intensely aware of it. Secular people share with relish stories about the foibles of Christians and churches they know. The media are equally searching in their scrutiny. Thus, an Adventism that confines itself largely to doctrine and things of the intellect is doomed to failure in a secular context. Its witness has already been fatally discounted before it occurs.

Although what you believe may have little impact on how you live, how you live has a *powerful* impact on what you believe. This is another major theme of the crucial chapter "Mind Cure" in the book *The Ministry of Healing*. The routine actions of daily life have a powerful effect on what people believe and how they feel and think.

Let me illustrate. I have a daughter who is now entering

adolescence. Until fairly recently she would, on occasion, pout with a whole heart. She would be sitting at the dinner table, and something or other would strike her wrong. Her whole face and body would twist up, and she would avoid all eye contact. I discovered that I could get her out of the pout with surprising ease. All I had to do was find a way to get her to smile. In the act of smiling, that miserable feeling—the whole attitude of pouting—just vanished. I would say, "What's that? You're not smiling, are you? Don't you dare smile! Do I see the corners of your mouth turning up?" Somehow that gets her every time—she cracks up! And when she does, the pout is gone, and she cannot seem to get it back, even if she tries! With my four-year-old, the magic words are, "Don't smile; your face might crack!"

Something similar can work with groups of adults as well. If a group you are speaking to has confidence in you, ask them to smile as big and broad a smile as possible. Give them a big smile and invite them to return it. Unless the audience is feeling some resistance toward the speaker, a group smile seems to make everyone feel better almost immediately. This is only an illustration. How we behave has a powerful impact not only on what we feel but on how we think and what we believe.

I know this sounds like manipulation—and to some that may be offensive. But I look at it this way. God made us the way He made us. He has put laws into our minds and hearts. Is it a bad thing to consciously choose to live in a way that will assist us in our walk with God and resist secular drift? If we know the things we need to do in order to stay close to God, why not do them? The reality is that *how you live has a powerful impact on what you believe.*

This is why evangelists like to call people up front. There is something about getting out of your seat and walking to the front that nails down a decision in a way that very few other things can do. In mentioning this, I should probably point out, however, that altar calls must not be handled in a way that compromises integrity and free choice. Secular people do not respond well to the traditional call in most instances. One must be careful not to unnecessarily violate social boundaries. So I normally try to find ways other than altar calls to seal decisions in the experience of secular people.

The one time in secular people's lives when you can make that kind of an appeal is when they attend a baptism. I am not sure how to explain that. But after baptizing people, I like to say something like, "Well, you've all seen what just happened; if you have never been baptized you may be thinking, 'My, I'd like to do that. I'd like to be fully devoted to God.' I'm not talking about baptizing you tomorrow or next week. But you'd like to learn what baptism means and what Christian life is all about. If you feel that way this morning, would you just stand for a minute?" I remember one time when I made such an appeal, and nineteen people stood up, half of whom I'd never seen before. I had sensed that it was a nonthreatening situation. It was part of a whole context in which the call was perceived as appropriate. People stood up who had just walked into the church for the first time! There is something about standing up at such times that solidifies a decision. It has to do with acting out our faith, even the first glimmer of faith.

The strongest safeguard against secularism—and even a secular psychologist will tell you this if you ask—is a seven-day-a-week religion. It's a faith that impacts in some way on every moment of every day of our lives. I was somewhat amused to discover that on many of the Caribbean islands, Adventists are known as "Seven Days." When I arrived for a camp meeting in the Bahamas, the newspaper declared, "Speaker Arrives for Seven Days Conference." I wish that were not just a misunderstanding but a statement of reality! Adventism cannot afford to be isolated in the closet of our experience. To be effective in a secular world, it must affect the whole of our experience.

When we talk about seven-day-a-week Adventism, we are talking about practicing the Seventh-day Adventist lifestyle. I realize that this gets us into something controversial. Many people have different opinions of what it means to live as a Seventh-day Adventist. But the point I want to make with absolute clarity is that without some kind of consistent practice of faith, secular drift is inevitable in one form or another.

For all its perceived flaws, the Adventist lifestyle that has been handed down to us is a superb example of a seven-day religion. When we shop for clothes, what are we—or should we—be doing? We are asking ourselves questions such as, "What impact will this clothing have on my witness for Christ? Will it aid or hinder my mission in life?" When we shop for groceries, we spend a lot of time reading labels. Why? Because we do not want to put into our bodies things that will clog up our minds and render us less fit for the difficult task of honoring God in all we do, say, or think. As a result, when we shop for clothing or groceries, we are constantly being reminded of God's claim on our lives.

When I make up the family budget each month, what do you suppose is on top of the list? Tithes and offerings. Everything that a Seventh-day Adventist does in life is potentially tied in with God in some way or another. And, rightly handled, this is a tremendous asset to faith in a secular world. I am not trying to tell you exactly what form the Adventist lifestyle should take in your case. But frankly, Adventism without consistent daily practice is not going to be maintained effectively in a secular world.

There are dangers in two extremes. A rigid lifestyle without a living relationship with God is drudgery. A devotional life without practice is also doomed to fail. Today in many families we have grandparents who believe in Adventism and practice the lifestyle, children who either believe without practice or practice the lifestyle without a clear understanding of what it means, and grandchildren who often throw the whole thing out. We desperately need to restore the unity of Adventist faith—not only holding certain ideas about God and Scripture, but also practicing a wholehearted, lifelong response to what Christ has done for us.

This wholehearted style of life is no denial of justification by faith. It simply recognizes that when Christ offers the gift, He also makes a claim. The great rallying cry of the first-century Christian church was "Jesus is Lord." To modernize that terminology a bit results in something like "Jesus is the Boss." When a first-century Christian said, "Jesus is Lord," he or she meant, "He has the right to tell me what to do and how to live." The relationship between justification and lordship is most effectively illustrated by a story Jesus told His disciples. In Matthew 18:23-35 a king forgives his servant a debt of ten thousand talents—perhaps ten billion dollars in inflated currency! It is assumed in the story that the servant would gladly respond by forgiving his fellow servant a debt of a mere one hundred days' wages. The story is a parable of divine and human forgiveness. What God does for us becomes a model for how we should treat one another. A balanced, living faith includes both devotion and action. We are saved by faith alone, but saving faith is never alone!

Not only is the Seventh-day Adventist lifestyle one of the best ways to maintain faith in a secular world; it offers a major side benefit as well: self-discipline. Self-discipline is rarely seen these days. Couch potatoes would love to be Michael Jordan or Joe Montana, but few realize what such athletes have to go through to attain excellence in their chosen field. Paul argues in 1 Corinthians 9 that our chosen spiritual field is worthy of a similar discipline. The

Seventh-day Adventist lifestyle was designed to enable people to function as peak-performance Christians. If you want to make a mark for Christ in the contest of life, discipline is the only way to go.

I am not suggesting a miserable, spoilsport lifestyle. Denying oneself the lesser things in life helps to guarantee that the greater things will get their proper attention. Take family budgeting as an example. Somebody once said that the cost of living is whatever you make plus 10 percent! Most people find that ridiculous assertion to be true. We all get used to whatever our income is, and then we want just a little bit more. Most people do not find it necessary to budget—when the money runs out, the party is over. But when you do that, your money goes to whatever comes up first. *The whole point about budgeting is to make sure the important things get cared for first.* I have known people who bought twelve boxes of Valentine candy before paying the rent, and then were unable to pay it. Then they would go to family and friends and say, "If you don't help me out, they'll throw me out on the street." And this pattern often repeats itself month after month after month.

Discipline means putting things that really matter first. Do you really want a roof over your head? You had better pay the rent first. Do you really want to eat? You'd better buy groceries before taking that trip to Hawaii.

So it is with spiritual things. *The main point of the Adventist lifestyle is to make sure that the most important matters in life get the greatest attention.* And that involves discipline.

While we are on this subject, let me make a point about lifestyle witnessing. If we expect to reach secular people, the Adventist lifestyle must be presented as a lifestyle of principle rather than just precept. Secular people are not looking for a list of rules with a dotted line on the bottom for their signature of blind compliance. They want to understand the reason behind lifestyle standards. "Why do you want me to do these things? Why is it that you don't want people to wear jewelry?" If there is no good reason for a standard, why have it? If there are sound reasons, why are they not clearer to contemporary people? Standards need to make sense to secular people. When we are dealing with them, we will have the *challenge* of defending the Adventist lifestyle as a viable principle. I think that on the whole it can be defended, but perhaps on slightly different grounds than we may have used in the past.

Secular people will point out to you, for example, that people who drink socially tend to live three years longer than people who don't, all other things being equal. Well, that should not be a surprise. Adventists are often known for being a little uptight. And a drink now and then does relax you some. But that does not impress me. Although often overlooked, Ellen White met such challenges on the basis of principle. A good example is *Testimonies to the Church*, volume 5, pages 354 to 361. She did not argue that alcohol is to be avoided because the Bible explicitly says so. She rather argued scientifically. For one thing, no one knows who might be an alcoholic. Social drinking, all other things being equal, may have a slightly relaxing effect, but alcoholism has a *devastating* impact on the alcoholic and everyone who is close to him.

But suppose you are a moderate social drinker, gaining all those supposed health benefits. Ellen White was still not impressed. She said that if you are an elder in the church and drank socially, you influenced others to drink. And if those you influence become alcoholics, who is responsible? Some people say they keep their social drinking a secret, but that introduces an element of deception and inauthenticity to one's Christian walk. To profess one thing and live another is not spiritually healthy.

A further consideration is research indicating that

every drink destroys some brain cells. I don't know about you, but I cannot afford to lose any brain cells. A fourth reason for avoiding alcohol is that alcohol especially tends to affect the will. But if you want to keep faith in a secular world, your will has to be charged up and ready to go twenty-four hours a day, seven days a week. I believe that when we rightly understand the genius behind the Seventh-day Adventist lifestyle—when we see that it is undergirded by common sense and based on reasonable principles, we can sell it to secular people. They won't buy into something just because we said so, or at first even because the Bible said so. They want to know, "Does it make sense? Is this really the way I want to live?"

One thing should be clear by now: The same life practices that maintain a Christian's faith in a secular world provide the spiritual setting into which secular people can be attracted to come. We cannot ask them to give up what we have not given up. Neither can we expect them to experience what we ourselves never experienced. Outreach to secular people begins with outreach to the secular mind-set in our churches and, above all, in our own hearts.

To share is to keep

A devotional walk with God and its consequences in everyday life are two *key* factors in maintaining faith in a secular world. There is at least one more. In order to keep our faith, it is necessary to share it. This is not true just today. It has always been a fact of spiritual life. In the Old Testament the key to bringing the power of God into the lives of His people was to recite over and over the things that He did for them in their past history.

Consider the plight of King Jehoshaphat. According to 2 Chronicles 20, he was under attack by the armies of three nations. As we would expect, he called his council together. But instead of developing a military or diplomatic strategy, he led them in prayer. How would you and I pray in that situation? Many of us would succumb to abject and pitiful pleading. But Jehoshaphat said, "Lord, You brought us out of Egypt with a mighty hand and an outstretched arm; You brought us through the wilderness. And when we got to the land as You promised us, there were hostile nations all around. You told us to leave them alone, and now they're coming against us. You took care of us then. You can do it again. Our eyes are upon You."

As Jehoshaphat was recounting the acts of God, instead of pleading abjectly in a desperate situation, the power of the Exodus experience was manifested again. Instead of a battle, the enemy armies were taken care of by a choir. They sang a song and blew them right out of town. The power of God that divided the Red Sea and fed them in the wilderness returned in response to Jehoshaphat's retelling of the Exodus. There is something about reciting what God has done for you in the past that brings the power of God back into your life. And if you regularly experience the power of God in your life, secularism can have no influence over you.

Expression deepens impression. Talk faith, and you will have faith. Ellen White expressed this idea forcefully in *The Ministry of Healing*:

> It is a law of nature that our thoughts and feelings are encouraged and strengthened as we give them utterance. While words express thoughts, it is also true that thoughts follow words. If we would give more expression to our faith, rejoice more in the blessings that we know we have,—the great mercy and love of God,—we should have more faith and greater joy. No tongue can express, no finite mind can conceive, the blessing that results from appreciating the goodness and love of God (251-253).

Can you remember a time when you shared your personal testimony with a friend or a stranger? You told of the helplessness of your human condition, but you also shared the excitement and joy that came with the discovery that if no one else in the universe had sinned, Christ would still have died for you. Whenever the cross of Christ is uplifted, the Holy Spirit presses the claim of the cross home with power to those listening. And that same power spills back to the one who testifies. Can you remember how the act of sharing your faith confirmed your own faith? It was like camp meeting all over again. I am rarely so confident and secure in my walk with God as I am when I share what He has done for me with others. The power of God's original working in my life is renewed in the retelling. This can be true even of preaching. Many a preacher has entered the pulpit discouraged and left it on fire! Share faith, and you will have more faith.

If these things are so, why do we witness as little as we do? One would expect that something as stimulating to faith as sharing it would be a centerpiece in our strategy. A major deterrent to sharing faith in a secular world is our sense that reaching out to others outside our faith circle oversteps the boundaries of social propriety. When we think of witness, we think of badgering people, intruding into their lives. The golden rule comes into effect here. "Do unto others as you would have them do unto you." I have spoken to hundreds of Adventists whose conscience bothers them about the way they try to share their faith. The result is miserable. Many Adventists feel guilty when they witness and guilty if they don't. That is no way to live.

We can be freed to witness again when we find out that *true* witness has two basic foundation principles that prevent us from overstepping the boundaries of social propriety. The first principle is that before you can get people to listen to you, you have to put them at ease. They need to be comfortable. In a secular environment, railing at somebody on a street corner may have the opposite effect from what we intend. Can you remember the last time you were confronted by a person who repeatedly told you what to do and put you down by highlighting his or her own superior understanding? Did you feel at ease in that person's presence? Did you feel like listening any further to what that person had to say? Did you want to become like him or her?

It is not necessary to put people down or to nag them in order to share your faith. Putting people at ease means that you avoid the attitude of a superior. It means relating to them in such a way that they are comfortable in your presence. It means that you spend more time listening than talking, at least at first. Jesus certainly had that ability, for prostitutes and sinners loved to be around Him. Witnessing in this way can be very difficult for Adventists in a secular world.

Putting people at ease may be a characteristic that is inherited as much as it is learned. I find it harder than some of my friends do. The good news is that we all can improve in the art of putting others at ease, and while some will always be more successful at it than others, training in interpersonal relationships is well worth the effort for any Christian who wants to reach out to secular neighbors, friends, and family.

The second principle of true witness is to live an attractive, Christ-centered style of life yourself. Most secular people are looking for something better, and when they see a person who "has her act together," they find it incredibly attractive. The funny thing is that most people *think* the TV stars have their act together. Although we know better, the visual medium is a powerful persuader. The stars smile and look permanently happy and charming, but the reality is that many of them can't wait to run home and shoot dope or commit suicide because they cannot face their real selves. Television is a fantasy image in a fantasy land.

Far more attractive than the painted-on smiles of the media is a person in real life who is making it work. People love to be with others who have their act together. They like people who listen to them and who don't put them down. Secular people are open to personal involvement in their lives by loving and lovable Christians who put people at ease and live Christlike, attractive lives.

You don't have to have a grit-your-teeth kind of determination to be a Christlike person. Grit-your-teeth people are very likely to be mean and selfish—the kind who tell others what to do and put them down. Christ-centered witnessing can come only from a life that is fully devoted to a living and active walk with God. From such a life, witnessing arises joyfully, not just dutifully.

Putting people at ease and being an attractive person reminds me of one of Ellen White's most humorous statements: "Let not your un-Christlike character misrepresent Jesus. Do not keep the little ones away from Him by your coldness and harshness. Never give them cause to feel that heaven would not be a pleasant place to them if you were there" (*The Ministry of Healing*, 43, 44). Coldness and harshness have a repelling influence rather than an attractive one. They are the opposite of true witness. I like to think that a good test for the attractiveness of my Christian walk is how children respond to me, both mine and others. Do children enjoy being around me, or do they tend to shy away fearfully? If you put children at ease, you are probably putting their parents and other adults at ease.

Let me illustrate by boasting about a good friend, Roland Hegstad, the editor of *Liberty* magazine. The first time Elder Hegstad came into my home and sat down in the living room, I was astonished. Within three minutes, all of my kids were in his lap. That told me more about his Christian character than all the articles and sermons I had appreciated through the years. My children immediately sensed that here was a person they could not only trust but who would be fun to be with. That's the way Jesus was—the minute He walked into a room, the kids were all mobbing about. The disciples tried to chase them away, but Jesus was having too much fun to permit that!

Speaking of the analogy between working with children and working with secular people, one of the interesting side benefits of this study for me has been a better understanding of how to help our children maintain faith in a secular world. It might be helpful to review briefly some of the most significant conclusions of the Valuegenesis study. The study concluded that there are six characteristics of homes and churches where young people tend to remain in the faith. Three of these characteristics pertain to the family. Families that have interesting family worships, in which the parents talk freely about their faith, and that engage the children in helping or service projects in the community, have a far higher rate of retention than families that don't have these three characteristics.

Three traits also show up in churches that keep young people in the faith. They have a youth program (Sabbath School and otherwise) that the youth themselves consider interesting. The youth also find that such churches offer a warm and accepting environment. And the youth feel that they have the freedom to question the faith and the things that are going on in the church. It is interesting that the same things that make our churches hospitable to secular people will also make them hospitable to our own young people.

Sharing our faith in the secular world is a major challenge. We not only need to learn a whole new way of expressing our faith, but we also need to learn how to do so without crossing social barriers that end the relationship. The main point of this chapter, however, is that sharing our faith is important, not only because secular people need Christ, but because we also need the spiritual strength and affirmation that come when we share our faith. Fortunately, although communicating the gospel in a secular world is a great challenge, it can be done. In the next section of the book we will examine the dynamics of outreach to secular people and explore methods that Adventists are using successfully in a number of places.

Part Three

Sharing Faith in a Secular World

8

The Basic Needs of Secular People

How can we share our faith in a secular world? How can we communicate with secular people in an effective way? How do we get past the many barriers that secular people erect in order to protect themselves against the unwanted influence of religion? A good way to start is to deal with secular people the same way Jesus dealt with people. He met them at the point of felt need—that place in their life where they were searching for something better.

> Christ's method alone will give true success in reaching the people. The Saviour mingled with men as one who desired their good. He showed His sympathy for them, ministered to their needs, and won their confidence. Then He bade them, "Follow Me" (*The Ministry of Healing*, 143).

Notice that in a series of five steps, Jesus left the direct spiritual appeal till last. He spent time with people, "mingling" in conversation, showing sympathy, meeting their needs, and winning their confidence before He felt comfortable challenging them with His unique mission. His method is still the best method. In this section we will try to put flesh on these suggestive hints by exploring some proven ways to meet secular people at the point of their felt need and move them into an acknowledgment of their real need for the gospel.

In this chapter we begin by examining the basic felt needs of secular people that come the closest to a direct spiritual interest and thus provide excellent openings for spiritual input. We will notice, as we explore these felt needs, the extent to which Adventism may attract or repel those who sense needs such as these.

A need for commitment

Secular people in a high-tech world generally feel a need for commitment to an issue or a person that is clearly greater than themselves. Although secular people may lack a commitment to organized religion, they nevertheless sense the need to commit themselves to something that transcends the ordinary in their existence. People cannot be satisfied with an endless round of routine tasks. Meaning must come from outside the ordinary.

People may seek to meet that need by a commitment to the Los Angeles Lakers, a political cause, or the good old U.S.A. in the Gulf War. The fate of a sports team may seem rather trivial as a center for one's life, but such attachments function as symbols directed toward a far more significant need—the need to be committed to something that is bigger than oneself. A much less trivial substitute for faith than athletics or even political concerns is the recent revival of interest in ecology. More and more people are committing themselves to recycling and reducing consumption so as not to overburden the environment. Protecting our planet is certainly a major and worthy concern, but I believe that people are searching for something even bigger than preserving the environment.

Adventism is uniquely positioned to make a difference

here. We can present the greatest Person and the greatest issues that anyone could possibly commit themselves to. The environment of the entire universe for all eternity is at stake in the work of the gospel. This makes sharing our faith one of the most meaningful tasks anyone could undertake. We can meet this need as we learn how to communicate the difference that Jesus makes in real, contemporary terms that touch base with life as it really is experienced today. We can meet this need as we learn how to tie in the issues of the great controversy to the issues that most people are talking about on a day-to-day basis.

Release from guilt

While secular people may feel uncomfortable with the term *guilt* in the context of biblical dos and don'ts, they will recognize the need for release from the failure to live up to their own highest expectations. Most persons, whether or not they know anything about the Ten Commandments, have a sense that they are not living up to what they expect from themselves, much less the standards that are held up to them from outside. In fact, when Catholics drop out of church to pursue secular interests, the thing they often miss most is the sense of release and forgiveness that came as a result of their participation in the confessional. Even nonreligious people need release from the sense of failure—the failure to achieve their hopes, their dreams, and their best intentions.

It is a fact of life that we inwardly expect of ourselves at least as much as we expect of other people. If I point my finger at you and say, "You shouldn't do that," what am I saying to myself? "Well, if I can pontificate about it to others, it certainly isn't right for me to do it."

And secular people often have a very strong sense of obligation, of where they want to be in life. The failure to achieve this leaves a sense of brokenness that cries out to be fixed. Many may deny the brokenness or drown it in alcohol, drugs, or promiscuity, but it can ultimately be fixed only at the cross. As Adventists, we need to ask the hard question of whether we truly understand and appreciate the cross. Until we do, we cannot meet this deep need, not only of secular people, but of all human beings. As we ourselves become forgiven people, we are enabled to minister forgiveness to others. On the other hand, it is impossible for an unforgiven person to be truly forgiving.

Genuine relationships

Secular people today have an urgent need for genuine relationships. They long for real relationships with real people who care enough to be honest as well as loyal. People today live noisy and distracted lives. They rush here and there, and relationships tend to be increasingly superficial. A committed Christian who is willing to enter into sensitive and authentic relationships with a selected number of secular people will find open arms waiting. As society becomes increasingly high-tech, the need for genuine relationships will increase. There will be a corresponding need for the caring touch, not so much physical as emotional and social.

The church has a tremendous opportunity here to reach out to struggling, hurting, secular people. Many have avoided church because of the perception that church people are inauthentic and superficial, and thus incapable of meeting their deep relational needs. But as a high-tech society makes it more difficult to maintain meaningful relationships, people are becoming open to a wider variety of options in their search for genuine relationships.

Many people deeply regret the loss of the extended family, where several generations along with cousins, aunts, and nephews all live in the same community and come together on a regular basis. These days brothers and sisters, parents and grandparents are scattered all over the country, and often all over the world. North American life is increasingly transient, with people moving wherever jobs or housing opportunities may take them. The church has the potential for providing a sense of extended family for those torn away from their own families of birth. A "welcome wagon" ministry targeting new arrivals to a community, for example, is one way to make contact with secular people, allowing them to consider the role the church could play in their lives. A loving Creator longs to use His people to reach out to a secular world with a loving and a caring touch, which the Holy Spirit can use to activate the even deeper need for the kind of relationship only God can provide.

Cosmic philosophy

Although they may not always be conscious of it, secular people have a need for a cosmic philosophy. Or, to put it in contemporary terms, they sense a need for social and cosmic interconnectedness. Human beings need to know that everything somehow fits together, that they belong to a meaningful and ordered universe. Adventists may not be conscious of this need because we often take our awareness of cosmic issues in the universe for granted. Just think what life would be like if you had no idea where you came from, no idea how the world is going to end, no idea what the universe beyond the telescope is like.

For Adventists, the whole great controversy scheme is a great organizing principle for our personal concept of the universe and our place in it. The average person looks out at the sky and has little or no idea what is going on out there. It is an empty void. All that is known is what can be perceived on earth by means of the five senses. What we call "eschatology," a cosmic philosophy that brings the whole universe into the equation, is foreign to most people.

At appropriate times, this sense of place in the larger scheme of things can be quite meaningful in a secular context.

Unorganized religion

Thus far this examination of the basic needs of secular people has proven to be quite encouraging for Adventist mission. Each of the first four needs can be answered by means of the resources found within our faith. In fact, as regards the first and fourth needs, there is no Christian group that is better positioned to make a difference in the secular world, provided we take the time and trouble to learn how to communicate these insights in a relevant way. The fifth need of secular people, however, is far more challenging to us. In harmony with the prevailing suspicion of authority in general comes a corresponding suspicion directed toward religious authority in particular. Secular people, therefore, tend to be opposed to what they often call "organized" religion. They fear coercion and the manipulation of their lives, sensing, perhaps, that religious coercion is the most vexing of assaults upon personal liberties. And, in fact, they are right. Thus, when secular people come to faith, they prefer to be involved in religious contexts where they are allowed considerable freedom and choice in the way they think and live. They like to be "involved" in the process by which they become converted.

We might as well be honest. Few Christian churches are more tightly organized and controlled than the Seventh-day Adventist Church. In my experience, structures and procedures that we often take for granted prove to be quite troubling as former secular people come in contact with them in a newfound Christian walk with us. We encourage people to become educated, for example, but then expect them to think freely only outside their involvement with the organized church. Fresh and creative ideas are frequently met with a "We never did it that way before," or "Ellen White says" (whether she in fact said it or not). It is not surprising that anti-organization secular people are often open to the nonsense of the New Age since New Age is, perhaps, the very epitome of unorganized religion.

The situation is not hopeless, however. I sense a rising openness among Adventist administrators to create more caring structures and interactions in relation to the local church. In an appendix to this book I will briefly share some ideas that may help reduce the barriers that secular people perceive as they encounter our organization. I have personally been able to blunt the negative impact of our organizational structure on secular people by an appeal to our church's history. We ourselves started out as an anti-establishment church. We broke ranks with all the other churches because they failed to follow the Bible, so our roots are in the radical reformation.

Perhaps we can recapture some of the radical spirit of our Adventist pioneers without losing all the positive benefits that competent organization can provide. Such an argument will come across lame, however, if you are not genuinely open to change yourself. If a local church is comfortable only with the ways they've done things in the past, secular people will not stay long because that is exactly the attitude they have been trying to avoid in their previous indifference to religion. This is an area that will require a great deal of sensitivity, both for Adventists who are comfortable in the church and for those outside whom we seek to attract. Helping former secular people discover and utilize their spiritual gifts is one way to demonstrate that there is plenty of room in God's house for individuality and creativity.

Another area of some advantage to Adventism is the secular attitude toward the Bible. A major barrier to reaching a secular person with the gospel is the mistaken ideas about the Bible that they have picked up. If you can disabuse them of these false ideas, they'll often be open to you. Many secular people think that the Bible teaches such unpalatable ideas as everlasting burning hell, child abuse, the subjugation of women and minorities, and administration by absolute fiat (as in the papacy). In the past, Adventists also left established churches because the conventional religious wisdom didn't correspond with what we found in the Bible. When secular people find out that the Bible isn't anything like they have been told, they are often quite open to its instruction.

Lifestyle direction

Secular people these days are earnestly seeking direction for their lifestyles. The number-one category of books that are selling today is self-help: self-help for plumbing, self-help for home repairs, self-help for marriage, self-help for potty training, etc. The big concern of most young people today is that they do not know what to do with their lives. The amazing openness of secular people to the bizarre absurdities of the New Age movement certainly indicates an openness to help from any direction, provided it touches base directly with felt needs and speaks a language that is familiar and meaningful.

Frankly, there is no faith anywhere that offers more direction for people's lifestyle than does the Adventist faith. We have suggestions for almost every area of life. I suspect that we do not always present it in a way that is effective or meaningful, but there is much there that would be of great interest in the secular context. As I mentioned in the previous section, if we can learn to think through and present lifestyle guidelines from a principled and logical perspective rather than as rigid rules, we have much that will be attractive to the average person on the street. But if we are not careful, we may present these things in a way that will cause the secular person to see all the red flags of "organized religion" in our approach.

Conclusion

This brief look at some of the basic felt needs of secular people indicates that Seventh-day Adventists have a marvelous opportunity to make major inroads into the secular community. In three of the six areas, we have a contribution to make that in some ways exceeds that of any other Christian group. In spite of this, we have made little or no impact in the secular world. This book is aimed at showing why this is so and offering suggestions to turn the situation around.

It would seem that the best approach for Adventists who wish to reach secular people would be to aim at the felt needs in the area of lifestyle, with particular emphasis on health, stress management, personal finance, and time management. There is already much material available on these matters. We can use these materials in two ways: as windows to help us understand how to communicate with the secular world and as sources of credible scientific support for the things we hold dear. However, we have a unique niche in this area in that we can integrate the help that people receive in specific areas into a comprehensive worldview (great controversy/cosmic eschatology) that will provide unity and meaning to every area of people's lives. This has been the strength of Adventism in each previous generation. We have a unified message with a unified world view. If we can learn to express our convictions in up-to-date language, we may be surprised at the people who will be anxious to get involved.

9

Cutting-Edge People

It clearly takes a special kind of person to reach out to secular people in a meaningful way without crossing the barriers of social propriety. What are the characteristics of such a person? To recall the starting point of this book, I would like to return to the concept of the "two-horizon" person. Every person has his or her own intellectual and social horizon, a perspective that is unique. The greatest need in our church is for two-horizon people—people who are comfortable not only in a traditional Adventist setting, but who can also step out and be comfortable in the secular world.

I know of no Seventh-day Adventist who fits that category better than Clifton Davis, the television actor. He was completely at home in the Adventist environment of Andrews University, whether mingling with students and teachers at the seminary, with Adventist administrators at the conference level, or in a local church. Yet he is equally at home in the public setting. I have seen him operate in a restaurant as it gradually dawned on the people around us that it was really him. Soon they started coming over with napkins and date books for autographs and a little conversation. He was sensitive to where each person was coming from, and what they expected from the encounter. It really inspired me to find more ways of making a difference for

Christ on airplanes and in routine business contacts.

The two-horizon person can make people feel at ease both in the church and in the world. Certainly any Adventist pastor who wants to work with secular people while pastoring a typical Adventist church will need a two-horizon perspective in order to survive. An independent ministry targeting a secular audience would be a much easier proposition than trying to do so within the context of pastoring an established Seventh-day Adventist church. But if secular people will be brought together with traditional Adventist people in your context, you will need a deep sensitivity to both groups. You cannot expect to railroad one group in order to accomplish something with the other. Such an approach will simply create a great deal of anger and heartache.

Identify with people

There are at least four qualities that equip a person to be effective in reaching secular people. First is the ability to identify with people, to sense where they are coming from. People with this quality are able to get close to others in a hurry, to intuitively put themselves in other people's shoes and see the world through their eyes.

I had a good friend named Joe who was pastoring in the same conference I was in. I always envied Joe's razor-sharp ability to zero in on a person and identify what was going on deep inside. I will never forget the time we were on the paint crew at the conference camp. One Sunday a number of church members came up from the city to help us out for a day. Around ten o'clock Joe was dropped off at our work site with the message, "He's here to help out." He immediately said, "Hi. My name's Joe," etc. After a couple of minutes' conversation, Joe found out that one young man had just come from Yugoslavia. "Are you here with your family?" he asked.

"No, no. My sister's still back there."

Suddenly Joe turned to him, looked him directly in the eye, and said, "You're worried about your sister, aren't you?" Immediately a tear came down the fellow's cheek. Joe continued, "Why don't we pray about her right now?" We all dropped to our knees on the dropcloth and prayed for this guy's sister.

Joe hadn't been in the room five minutes!

Adventists, mirroring the nineteenth-century heritage of the American frontier, tend to be rugged individualists. This individualism is reflected in the proliferation of private interest groups at the fringes of Adventism today. The individualist attitude says, "If people see things differently than we do, it's their problem." But spiritual outreach across cultural lines requires great sensitivity to other people's ideas and feelings.

If you realize that you have difficulty identifying with people, take it to the Lord. By the Spirit, many Christians can become specially "gifted" in order to enhance the spiritual power of their ministry to others. But even those who do not feel "gifted" can learn to identify with people more effectively with a little training and practice. Make it a project to learn from your mistakes. The neat thing about secular people is that they are very forgiving of relational mistakes, *if* you are honest and genuine. Secular people do not appreciate the person who is "holier than thou." But if you make an honest mistake in relating to a secular person, just say, "I really blew that!" "I don't know why I said that," etc. You will be amazed at how forgiving they can be. They are usually quite willing to teach you how to talk to them if you give them an honest effort.

Not all of us are as naturally gifted as Joe. I certainly am not. I have to struggle to put people at ease. But this is one of the most important things that any of us can learn in this life. It is worth making a top priority. As I have repeatedly pointed out, secular ministry is not for everybody. But those who feel the call of God to make a difference in the secular environment will want to sharpen their ability to identify with people and understand the inner drives that motivate their behavior.

Creative witness

The second quality that sets two-horizon people apart is the ability to offer a fresh and creative witness when the circumstances demand it. A canned or prepackaged approach is limited in its impact to those who are interested in what that particular kind of can contains. Examples of a canned approach would be a set of Bible lessons that is given to everyone regardless of background or interests, or an evangelistic series that is identical in every community regardless of its ethnic or social setting. With secular people, it is necessary to "wing it" a lot more than most of us are accustomed to. Fresh and creative witness means you are able to say things that you have never said anywhere else but you can say them now because the situation requires it. Obviously, the only way we can do this is to be sensitive to the leading of the Holy Spirit. The Spirit can impress you in particular circumstances to offer the right word at the right time, much as Jesus did while He was here on earth.

I remember an occasion where the Spirit helped me to "wing it" in an effective way. A woman in my church had been an Adventist for a long time. She married a man who had no background in Adventism whatsoever, and she did little to enlighten him during their courtship. She was in her fifties, and he was somewhat older. Some time after the marriage, she requested that I visit her and meet her husband. They lived in a lovely mountainous area about one hundred miles from my urban church. I thought, "Well, let me make a nice day of it and refresh myself in the countryside as I go up for the visit."

As I approached the area it was raining, foggy, and cloudy. I reached their lakeside home, parked the car, and got out. There on the lawn was one of these big yard umbrellas, and there sat Joe, the husband (no relation to Joe the pastor), with two of his friends, drinking hard liquor in the rain. I thought to myself, "Pastor, this is going to be one of those days!" The Adventist wife was nowhere to be seen, so I went over and sat down at the table. I introduced myself as the pastor of the wife's church.

"Yes, we've been expecting you," Joe said, and he immediately picked up the bottle of brandy that was on the table, handed it to me, and said, "Have a drink, pastor."

This was the moment of truth for our relationship. To mishandle this moment could put an end to any hope of reaching this man. Unfortunately, I often blow such opportunities; I have a hard time handling people right. But on this occasion, I believe the Lord put words in my mouth. Although I had never met this man, I took the bottle of brandy, looked at it, and said, "Oh, that's good brandy. But, I'm interested in something a little stronger right now."

I had his full attention. He leaned forward and said, "Something stronger than brandy?"

"Yeah," I said, "I'd like the strongest drink in the world."

He said, "What's that?"

I said, "It's a drink that is so strong, it'll float a battleship. I'd like a glass of water."

Joe was on the lawn, rolling with laughter. He was laughing so hard that it took about fifteen minutes to get him back together again. We were friends from that moment on. A little while later we had dinner together, along with his wife and the two neighbors. When the dinner was over, I said, "You know, I need to be going back, but, Joe, would you mind if I prayed for you before I go?" Now I would not make such an offer in every circumstance, but I felt impressed that this was the right thing to do on this occasion. Joe said, "Sure." And I began to pray for him, for his neighbors, and his family. In the middle of the prayer, I heard a noise. It was a cross between panting and sniffling. I might as well admit it, I peeked. And Joe was just sobbing and sobbing. When I finished the prayer, he continued sobbing for half an hour. No one had ever prayed for him. And shortly after that he began coming to church in spite of the distance.

Let me be very honest with you. I don't have successes like this all the time. In fact, I might be shooting 20 to 30 percent at best. But on that one occasion, a fresh and creative witness reached a person who had never been touched before. Fresh and creative? I would never have dreamed that a joke about alcohol would be the way into a person's heart. But if the Spirit is with you and your heart is sensitive to people, you can often sense the right word at the right time, even when you do not know the people very well.

I think that is the way Jesus would have handled it. He went to many kinds of parties, and sinners were never embarrassed by His presence. He found a way to make them feel at home, and, at the same time, maintain those limits that were necessary to His own spiritual experience. Fresh and creative witness means a willingness, when necessary, to approach people and issues from an entirely different angle than you have ever tried before.

Biblical knowledge

A third quality that is absolutely essential in the person who desires to witness effectively to secular people is to know the Bible well. This is a tough one. It certainly does not happen overnight. But a thorough knowledge of the content of the Bible is critical. Secular people ask questions that you have never dreamed of. They almost never ask the questions that are found in the typical set of Bible lessons. When secular people see a bumper sticker that says "Jesus is the Answer," they say, "What was the question?" They are not asking Christian types of questions.

Most of our traditional Bible lesson sets were designed to persuade people who already know Christ and are familiar with their Bibles. Secular people find it difficult to relate to that kind of biblical knowledge.

To know the Bible well is to be prepared so that when an off-the-wall question comes, you can reorient your biblical knowledge in relation to the question and provide an answer from Scripture that transcends anything you knew before. That may seem an impossible task, but you must not allow the enormity of it to slow you down. If you have no idea how to answer, just say, "That was a great question! Hey, do you mind if I go home and think about it for a while? A question as good as that deserves a solid answer. Give me a little time, and I'll get back to you." As we noted earlier, secular people are a lot more forgiving than we might expect. They do not expect you to have all the answers at the tip of your fingers. In fact, they will likely become suspicious if you imply that you do!

My favorite style of evangelism is what I call "open forum." An open forum lets people interrupt any time to ask questions or offer comments. It is not a great deal different from the "Donahue" or "Oprah Winfrey" shows on television. Secular people found my open forum presentations entertaining as well as challenging. They would say, "This is better than television. I would come here every night of the week." Apparently, the give and take of intellectual debate remains the object of tremendous interest. The challenge of open forum, of course, is that you never know what you are going to face, so you had better know your Bible and be sensitive to the Spirit's guidance. I remember a Jewish woman who would regularly blurt out, "I don't believe that!" I would respond, "You don't believe it? Why not?" I would let her talk a little bit; then I would say, "What do you think of this text here?" It was amazing how this style built rapport with a fairly secular audience. But in an open forum setting, the lack of a thorough knowledge of the biblical material will often leave you speechless.

Common language

The fourth quality that characterizes Christians who successfully interact with the secular environment is the use of basic, everyday language in outreach efforts. There is a language that is common to all who speak English, the language used in magazines like *Newsweek* and the daily newspaper. These media use a basic eight thousand to ten thousand words that communicate to virtually everyone whether or not they can read or write. We Adventists, on the other hand, often use our own "in-house" language that communicates accurately only among us.

Just imagine a secular person visiting an Adventist church for the first time. On the platform is a person doing a special feature on investment. What will the secular person be thinking? "Hey, these people must be into stocks and bonds. I bet they're loaded." Someone else then gets up and says, "You know, I'll never forget the day I finally saw the light." Light? What light? A Bud Lite?

The reality is that most Adventists who are educated and work in white-collar jobs know how to talk to secular people on a day-to-day basis. The problem is that we tend to segregate that language to the secular part of our lives and switch to a different language whenever we want to express our spiritual needs and concerns. We should challenge each other to express spiritual feelings in everyday language within the church so that it will become second nature when we reach outside to others.

As a pastor in New York City, one of the intellectual

capitals of the secular world, I went out of my way to screen my sermons with this in mind. I would ask myself at every step, "What sense would this language make to somebody coming in off the street? How can I make it as basic and as clear as possible without giving up content?" I gradually learned that you can talk about complex things without using complex language. It takes time to learn. I remember with much regret the time a Lutheran couple came to my church and I prepared a sermon on the law "just for them." I had not made it to the ten-minute mark of the sermon before I realized that I had totally blown it, but I did not know what to do to redeem the situation. They never came back.

It has taken me years to learn the use of common language, and then it took a few more years to start overcoming the impact of Ph.D. studies on my vocabulary. But the more we learn to use the language that all people have in common, the wider our impact can be on a diverse audience. Both the intellectual and the illiterate are reached by the same message.

Conclusion

The four qualities described briefly above require both involvement with the Holy Spirit and much effort and experience. It is not necessary, however, to master all these areas before one can begin reaching out to secular people. The good news is that God enables those whom He calls. If you feel called to develop an outreach to secular people, I invite you to commit yourself before God to get the training and experience that will make a difference in the quality of your efforts. The very best training, however, lies in the doing.

10

The Practice of One-to-One Outreach

The preceding chapter concludes by putting a finger on what is, perhaps, the greatest Adventist shortcoming in dealing with secular people: our failure to learn and use language and terminology that is meaningful to their experience. How do you learn their language? The same way children learn language—by listening and talking. As we interact regularly with secular people we will learn how to communicate effectively with them.

How does this work in practice? How do you actually get close to a secular person?

I know of no better way than what I call "creative listening." Creative listening is the art of asking leading questions that gently and kindly zero in on what really matters in the other person's life. Creative listening is hard for me. I tend to talk too much, and I sometimes talk myself right out of a conversation. The goal of creative listening is to sensitively encourage a person to reveal those things that are of greatest concern in his or her life at the time. My friend Joe rarely needs more than five questions before he discovers the central area of need in a person's life. I must confess that I wish I were equally gifted in this area.

Creative listening means learning to ask the right question at the right time. When you try it, though, you will quickly learn that privacy is a major issue with secular people. It is easy to overstep their bounds and embarrass yourself by pushing too hard or too fast. Keep in mind that this will happen to you as you reach out to secular people. You will often say the wrong thing and offend people as you search to find what makes them tick. But failure is probably the best way to learn anything. At Greenfield Village, the attendant at Thomas Edison's laboratory told us Edison made 3,573 attempts before he made the first usable light bulb. Along the way, someone asked Edison how he felt about his thousands of failures. He replied, "I now know that many ways *not* to make a light bulb!" Failure is a marvelous path to learning! Certainly the spread of the gospel is worthy of Edison's entrepreneurial spirit.

But it is one thing to experiment on light bulbs and another to experiment on people. Most of us are naturally reluctant to overstep the comfort zone of others. Fortunately, as was mentioned earlier, secular people appreciate someone who's honest and open, someone who says, "Oh, I think that was the wrong thing to say," or "Sorry, I blew that one." As long as we do not wear our feelings on our sleeve, communicating with secular people will be a great adventure. In light of what the cross tells us concerning our standing with God, we can learn to place the natural tensions of everyday relationship in their proper perspective.

Someone once objected, "Didn't Jesus zero in right to the point with the rich young ruler? He didn't waste time with a lot of fancy listening." That was often true in Jesus' experience. The difference between Jesus and me, however, is that Jesus could read the heart. I can't do that yet. If I ever learn how, it will come as the result of a lengthy two-step process. First, I must remove any barriers that may prevent His Spirit from impressing me regarding others. Second, I need to spend a lot of time in creative listening. The experience with Joe's brandy is the exception. Most strangers cannot be understood without much listening.

Nothing in this book is intended to minimize the role of the Spirit in outreach, but we must not forget the point of chapter 1: God does not normally bypass the human process of learning. We have a major role to play in cooperating with God. He has more than one purpose in this. For one thing, as we go through the laborious process of learning how to sense what is in the heart of people on the street, we will learn lessons about ourselves that can be learned no other way. If it had been better in the ultimate scheme of things for angels to do the work of outreach, they would gladly do it. But God takes the risk of giving us the task, because it is as crucial to our well-being as it is to those we minister to.

A second purpose God has in allowing us to stumble on in our attempts to reach people is that such listening is a marvelous way to demonstrate Christlike love. Notice the words of John Stott:

> Dialogue is a token of genuine Christian love, because it indicates our steadfast resolve to rid our minds of the prejudices and caricatures which we may entertain about other people; the struggle to listen through their ears and look through their eyes so as to grasp what prevents them from hearing the gospel and seeing Christ; to sympathize with them in all their doubts, fears, and hangups.[1]

As any successfully married couple knows, love and listening are two sides of the same coin.

Apparently even Bible writers like John did a great deal of listening before writing down what God shared with them. For example, although God's word creates the world in the Old Testament, nowhere is "the Word" ever described as a divine person. Yet just such a figure was a prominent part of Greek philosophy. In Platonic thought "the Word" was a divine person who created and sustained the world and now serves as the mediator between God and humanity. So when John 1 talks about "the Word made flesh," it was as if John were proclaiming to the Greeks, "This 'Word' whom you worship, I declare unto you, is Jesus Christ!" John had learned, under the guidance of the Spirit, how to present the gospel effectively to the Greeks by careful attention to the way they thought about God.

Students of Revelation, therefore, will be quite interested to discover that Hekate, the most popular goddess of Asia Minor in the first century, was described in language much like the Revelator's description of Christ in Revelation 1. She was called the first and the last, the beginning and the end. She held the keys of heaven and hell and was able to reveal to people what went on in those places. To the Greeks of Asia Minor, John offered a Jesus that met their deepest longings in language that was meaningful to them. Even if we suppose that God was the source of the connections, it reminds us that the gospel can be heard only when it comes in context! As human beings we become familiar with people's context by listening!

The point of contact

Creative listening, therefore, is the starting point for outreach to a secular world. Whether you are seeking out individuals or want to hold evangelistic meetings in an area, there is no better way to begin the process than through listening. What are we looking for as we are listening? We are trying to discover the felt needs that open that person to input from others at that point in his or her experience. What are the needs that motivate that person's search for truth and self-betterment? Where is that person hurting? What problems stimulate a desire for something better?

There can be, of course, a difference between genuine needs and felt needs. All people have needs that they are not aware of, the greatest of all being, of course, to know Christ. But most people are not aware of their need for Christ, and they would deny their need for the gospel. So the starting point must be to aim at the needs they *do* feel. This approach is in harmony with a very basic human characteristic. James Engel points out in his book *Contemporary Christian Communication* that *every human being has a built-in barrier against persuasion*. Human beings have a natural aversion to changing their minds. And it is a good aversion. If we didn't have it, we would all change religions every day. We would all believe the latest thing we were told. There are people who do not have a very strong barrier against persuasion. You have no doubt met some. They jump from one idea to the next and never quite settle on anything. They are known as credulous or easily duped. Paul said they are "blown here and there by every wind of teaching" (Ephesians 4:14).

Most people, however, have a strong barrier against persuasion. They do not lightly change their minds on any topic. When somebody else comes along with an idea that is radically different from what they believe, what happens? A psychological brick wall goes up. And the more you pound against that wall, the more it is reinforced. But there is a way around those "brick walls." It is to approach people in the area of their felt needs. A felt need is a point in a person's life where he or she is open to instruction. Students of world mission call this felt need the point of contact, that point in a person's or a group's experience where an aspect of the gospel intersects with conscious needs and interests.

Let me illustrate. Not long ago, my biggest felt need was

to learn how you get babies that like a warm feeling in their pants to do what they are supposed to do in the place in which they are supposed to do it. That was a real felt need in my life for a time. We tried all kinds of angles, yet a particular child seemed to prefer doing it his way. At that point I was wide open to anyone with a suggestion I had not heard before, no matter how crazy the suggestion sounded at first! Several people said, "I had a kid just like that, and here's what worked for me." My wife and I were all ears. We gave these people our full and immediate attention. Regardless of how nutty their ideas were, we tried each one at least once, because we felt a huge need to resolve that problem. We were definitely interested in fresh and creative ideas on the subject.

If someone had come to me at that time (someone did) and asserted, "The beast of Revelation is Ronald Wilson Reagan, who has six letters in each of his three names," I would have been quite resistant. That would have made no sense to me in the light of what I know about Revelation. Furthermore, I would have had no interest in that person's opinion. So there! But someone approaching at the point of my felt need would have gotten a much more positive reaction. The barrier against persuasion would have come down immediately.

Secular people are no different. When you approach them at the point of their felt needs, they are wide open to instruction. They are searching for information on that very point.

I am reminded of the blood-pressure screening/food-sharing van ministry in New York City that most Adventists are now familiar with. Back in the 1970s people coming onto a van to get their blood pressure checked were invited on a registration sheet to check if they were interested in studying the Bible. One out of twenty or twenty-one would do so. But when they were asked in a soft-sell way if they would like to receive Bible studies, the ratio jumped immediately to one out of three! Some time after this the van team noticed that an even higher percentage of people seemed interested in material on how to manage stress. Would Bible-study guides on how to manage stress in one's life meet a felt need in New York City?

Standing on the corner of Forty-seventh Street and Sixth Avenue is an experience you will get nowhere else on earth. There are subways rumbling under you, buses roaring beside you, planes overhead, buildings seventy stories high by the dozen in all directions; within a stone's throw from where you stand, fifty thousand people are active and operating, seemingly shouldering past you all at once. Within fifty miles are more than twenty million! The energy of midtown Manhattan is incredible. But along with that adrenalin surge comes stress. By the end of the day you are exhausted! To make it worse, you go to bed, and your mind is spinning all the more. You are all keyed up. Stress is, therefore, the number-one felt need of people in New York City (and in many other parts of North America these days as well!).

Bible lessons on how to manage stress were developed entitled *Power to Cope*. The percentage of people accepting Bible studies skyrocketed as soon as the lessons were available. Now *85 to 87 percent* are accepting and continue to accept lessons; Jewish, Catholic, Muslim, it does not seem to matter. People are told, "We have a free set of Bible-study guides on how to cope with stress. Are you interested?" They just grab them, sometimes taking extra ones for all their friends.

One day on Wall Street there was a major felt need. Perhaps it was one of those days with a major downswing, but on that day 242 people came on the van in front of the stock exchange, and every single one accepted Bible studies. That's 242 out of 242! It must have been a very bad day on Wall Street. But that is what happens when you meet felt needs. The barrier against persuasion is gone. The key to opening up secular people to the gospel is to find a felt need and speak directly to it.

It is appropriate, in the light of Part Two of this book, to mention that the leaders of the van ministry always insist that the key to the successes of the program are due more than anything else to the outpouring of the Holy Spirit in response to prayer and the prayer-filled lives of the those serving on the vans. Thus, the two key points of this book are clearly illustrated by the van ministry. Ministry to secular people will succeed only in an atmosphere of God's presence and power, on the one hand, and of sensitivity to people's needs on the other. Prayer without an understanding of method will work wonders. But even more powerful is a ministry that combines prayer with intelligent sensitivity to how secular people can be best approached. Prayer is a constant practice in the van ministry. But when prayer was combined with skillful personal invitations, and with lessons that met felt needs, interest increased from 5 percent to 85 percent and more!

Frankly, however, the felt-need principle makes a Christian's life more complex because secular people are as diverse as snowflakes. Talk to twenty secular people, and you will discover twenty different felt needs that you have never met in quite that form before. Without a fresh and creative approach, the situation may appear hopeless. But although the attempt will have its ups and downs, it is a great adventure that will enrich the life of everyone who thrives on adventure.

Door-to-door listening

How does the felt-need principle operate on a large scale? How do you do this as a church? I would suggest what I call door-to-door listening. We approach people door to door for a wide variety of reasons. Why not door-to-door listening? A simple way to accomplish this is to target a specific geographical area or a particular socioeconomic segment of the target area. Andrews University can, if needed, provide demographic breakdowns according to the zip codes in your area. (The address of the Institute of Church Ministry is found in the bibliography at the end of this book.) Create a short survey that attempts to discover what particular felt needs are abundant in the target community. As early returns from the survey come in, it is important to modify the survey itself on the basis of feedback. As areas of interest emerge, the local church or group can assess which of the felt needs they are in a position to address.

A group of us once did this in the South Bronx. No doubt you have heard about the South Bronx. It is a part of New York City that looks a lot like Sarajevo after another artillery bombardment. We were taking the survey on a block that had garbage in the street, broken glass in the empty lots, burned-out buildings, and a few high-rises that were hanging together by a thread. We went down the street taking surveys of what the felt needs of that community were. The author of the questionnaire developed an interesting set of questions, including, "Do you feel good about the condition of this block?" One hundred percent of the people said No. They did not feel good about the way their neighborhood looked. The next question asked, "If someone takes the lead in cleaning up the block, will you help?" To our amazement, 90 percent said Yes in an area that is known for apathy.

Was that block begging for a doctrinal crusade? Or was the ideal starting point a call for a person with a Christlike heart to move into that block and get involved? Such a person could encourage the people to galvanize the resources there—to clean up the empty lot, plant flowers, provide security, etc. It could be done. Most people are afraid to take the lead. But if someone took the lead, people would follow.

Meeting a felt need like this would create a great deal of interest in what else the church had to offer. There are physical dangers in such a response, of course, but that need not be a major barrier. God has programmed some people in a way that they don't get excited about tasks unless there is a measure of risk or adventure associated with them. Regardless of the type of neighborhood, when you take surveys door to door, you are looking for fertile fields, for people who are open to the kinds of things the church is able to offer. And when felt needs emerge, the Spirit will move believing hearts to take action!

Patience

Patience is necessary when working with secular people. The move from a totally secular environment into a traditional Adventist environment is not going to happen in two or three weeks. In my experience it averages about two years. What we are talking about here is long-term commitment, and this may be more appropriate to elders than to pastors in some circumstances. The key people who develop a relationship with a secular person need to be around when he or she goes all the way with Christ.

I remember one couple that I baptized. I officiated at their wedding and then baptized them a year later. On the day of their baptism the members were shocked. They thought the couple were already members of the church. They had been out Ingathering; they came to all the work bees; they went to all the prayer meetings—they were at everything. They were as active and involved in the church as anyone could be. But it was two years before they were comfortable in making a total commitment to Christ in the context of the Adventist Church. They insisted, "We want to know what we're getting into first. We plan to become Seventh-day Adventists, but we are going to become Seventh-day Adventists when we understand *all* that that means."

In dealing with secular people, there will be rough times along the way. One day the husband, who worked for IBM, came up to me with an issue of *Spectrum* magazine. He asked, "Does this have anything to do with Adventism?" In it were some articles about the Davenport fiasco and similar problems in the church. My heart was sinking fast! I just sat down with him and said, "Look, this church is not perfect. Administrators make mistakes, churches make mistakes, people and pastors make mistakes. If you're looking for perfection, you're looking in the wrong place. You can't find it on this planet. But," I said, "there's one thing I like about being an Adventist with all of the shortcomings, and that is that we are encouraged to keep growing in our understanding of truth, however long it takes. We are not content to settle down with tradition."

The husband's response was, "Yeah, that doesn't bother me."

Now you may think I fudged just a little, but I do believe what I said there in principle. I am a Seventh-day Adventist because I believe that we as a people are open to clearer expressions of truth. We are not as a people willing to settle into the rut of tradition. Maybe you don't think we are really open to change, or maybe you are satisfied with things the way they are. I believe, however, that there is much more God wants to reveal to us. The path of truth is like a shining light getting brighter and brighter until it reaches the ultimate goal. And we are not there yet. If we refuse to grow in grace and in understanding, we may find ourselves left behind as God turns to others.

The period I worked with this couple was also known to some as the "Ford crisis." It was a very traumatic time to be a pastor. When the youth caught wind of some of these things, they demanded a meeting to learn what was going on. I did the democratic thing and allowed them to set the agenda and bring all their friends. In retrospect, that was quite stupid. When meeting time came, not only were all the fifteen nonchurched people whom I was working with sitting in the front row, but thirty Adventists whom I had never seen before had come from other churches. And a couple of conference officials showed up as well!

The questions were very specific, and they came so thick and fast that there was no time to work through the issues from a biblical perspective. I could only give a short answer and go on. But most interesting to me was the fact that not one of those secular people was the least bit disturbed about the issues raised at that meeting. They said, "It's neat the way people in your church are so open and willing to discuss problems. This is the kind of place I want to be." What I did not have the heart to tell them then was that the conference president got twelve threatening phone calls from the unknown Adventists at that meeting. They did not know me and had no context for understanding what I was saying. They just did not like what was happening.

The conference president got me on the phone and said, "You had *some* kind of meeting there Sabbath, didn't you?"

I said, "Yeah."

He said, "I got all kinds of phone calls. Some people are pretty upset."

"Yeah, I guess I had some people there who don't know me very well. I guess airing some of those things was not particularly thrilling to them."

The president responded, "I have always had confidence in you. Let me suggest that you not have any more meetings like that."

My response was, "Don't worry. I have no plans to do

something like that ever again."

Let me share with you some things I learned from this experience. For one thing, there is a dark side to the open forum style. It is not realistic to expect that things will always go perfectly. It helps, however, to target your audience carefully whenever possible. As we noticed in Part One, church growth and reaching the unreached are two different processes. Meetings that attract and interest secular people may be very distressing to some of your own church people. That is simply a reality. I know that when I speak to an Adventist audience I speak differently than when I know I'm speaking to a secular audience. When an Adventist wonders why I said something in an unfamiliar way, I say, "Listen, I'm talking to them, not you. But if you have any problems, just ask me, and I will be happy to share it with you in your language." It certainly helps in such a situation if the Adventists in the audience know you personally and have confidence in your ministry.

Another way to handle the problem is to limit the audience by careful targeting. The meeting that got me in trouble had a hybrid target that attracted a mixed audience. Since the two audiences would each respond positively to a completely different approach, it left me with the task of deciding which to offend, and I decided that the church members would have to be the ones to handle it if necessary. A certain amount of flak is unavoidable in secular ministry, if Paul's experience is any guide!

Another lesson I have learned about open forums concerns dealing with Adventist "hot potatoes." When you are discussing biblical "hot potatoes," it is best to take the Word and work things through carefully with people who have questions. Stick to the Word and say only what is in the Word, and neither the right nor the left wing will trouble you much. Let the Word of God gradually transform people's thinking. Elevate the discussion by using biblical language instead of buying into the language of the debate. On hot issues such as the nature of Christ and the order of salvation, people may use unbiblical concepts or even biblical terms in a way that they are not used in the Bible.

Unless you have time to lay out the full biblical perspective, the best open forum answer may be, "I have problems with both sides on that issue. Keep in mind that each is trying to protect something that is true, so learn wherever you can, but don't believe everything you hear or see in print." I usually add that when we have time, we can take a closer look at that issue. I may also point out a Bible text that well illustrates the biblical tension between the two sides of the question, and then go back to my central topic.

But the lesson from my unhappy meeting that I find most pertinent to our purpose in this book is that secular people, rather than being turned off by the fact that the church isn't perfect, are usually excited that we are willing to openly acknowledge and discuss our imperfections. They say, "At least you guys don't think you have all the answers."

There was a time when Adventists thought that the only effective way to do evangelism and witnessing was by having absolute confidence in the rightness of our convictions. People would be swayed by the certitude of the one who was presenting the gospel to them. And that is true for a lot of people, including some secular people of the blue-collar variety. Many people are still looking for someone to tell them exactly what to do. But that approach usually backfires with the more educated secular types.

Mass media advertising has led to a situation where educated secular people have difficulty believing anything that is offered in the public square. Propaganda is not interested in truth, only in persuasion. Thus when an individual makes a strong statement about the certainty of his or her belief in the secular environment, he or she is automatically suspect. Basic to reaching the secular mind, therefore, is an attitude of honesty and openness to discovery. Secular people are attracted to those who are willing to admit that their understanding of truth is subject to limitation and distortion. The open forum setting is actually much more persuasive for them than an assertive lecture. Through listening and dialoguing, we show respect for the viewpoints of others, and this encourages a similar respect in return. Such an approach will require patience, however, as secular people do not normally experience rapid conversions to Christian faith.

Educated, white-collar secular people are not usually looking for the "true church." What they *are* delighted to find is a community that is fully devoted to an open, honest, and continuing search for truth. Those who know God's Word will not avoid giving that impression, for we know that "we see through a glass darkly" (1 Cor. 13:12), and that our knowledge of truth will continue to grow until the end (see Prov. 4:18).

Conclusion

This "how-to" chapter has been necessarily sketchy and suggestive, outlining only basic principles. Many will want specific ideas on how to approach secular people effectively. The best book I have ever read on the subject is James Engel's *Contemporary Christian Communications*. Since it is now out of print, I share some of the most helpful suggestions from that book in an appendix. Particularly useful is Engel's chart on the spiritual decision process. This chart helps the creative listener to pinpoint the level of spiritual interest in another person. Those interested in further "how-to" ideas on personal witnessing are directed to the appendix.

---

1. Quoted in James F. Engel, *Contemporary Christian Communications: Its Theory and Practice* (Nashville: Thomas Nelson, 1979), 60.

11

Outreach as a Church

The preceding chapter clearly shows that we cannot reach out to secular people in a vacuum. At some point we must confront the inevitable tension that lies between the way the church does things and the way secular people respond. We have to struggle with the question of how the Adventist horizon and the secular horizon can come together without compromising the best qualities of either. What can a local church or conference do to make a bigger impact in the secular environment?

Education

First we need to educate our own people in a number of areas. We need to teach them the need for a strong devotional life in a secular environment. The principles outlined in Part Two of this book can provide a starting point for such education. We also need to educate them about the importance of the Adventist lifestyle. Rather than helping evangelism, lowering standards hinders it. It is the "secularized" churches that are in decline. When secular people look for a church, they often pick the most demanding ones. So to be conservative in the area of lifestyle is not a negative unless it is combined with a rigid and judgmental attitude. A principled approach to lifestyle brings the divine into practical, everyday existence.

We also need to educate people about the problem of horizons to help them understand that without a lot of listening and learning they will be ineffective in reaching secular neighbors, friends, and family. In the process it is helpful to point out that the Bible does not offer a single, rigid model for outreach and evangelism. There are at least two great models of ministry, the fortress and the salt. Since most human beings are uncomfortable with change, it helps a great deal when we can see that opening ourselves up to change in the area of outreach will bring us into conformity with Scripture rather than the reverse.

Multiple ministries

As part of the process of education, we need to encourage a multiplicity of ministries. Secular people are as diverse as snowflakes. They are not normally reached in large groups. Each secular person tends to respond in a unique way. The only way, therefore, to counter the pluralism of society is with the pluralism of the Holy Spirit, which is an explosion of all kinds of outreach ministries empowered by the Spirit. This will not come from central planning, but from the members discovering the unique roles God has developed for each person. I am encouraged, therefore, by the spiritual gifts movement in our church. People are becoming interested in how the Holy Spirit has provided a unique mix of abilities to every Christian. No two people are gifted in exactly the same way. If secular people are as diverse as snowflakes, we need a missionary force that is as diverse as snowflakes. This is exactly what the Holy Spirit provides; every Christian discovering the unique niche where he or she can serve best.

Service is filled with joy and excitement whenever it flows not only from the gifts of the Spirit, but also from that unique burden or passion that God gives each person for ministry. Every person has a special passion for something. When a Christian ministers in the area of his or her passion, both maximum usefulness and personal fulfillment are attained. Many Adventists who I know have a consuming passion for New York City. Other people have a heavy burden for a particular ethnic group or a particular class of society such as the handicapped or the wealthy. Others have a passion for the environment. I suppose it would be safe to say that I have a passion for the unchurched and for those who have become disenchanted with conventional religion. If you have a life's passion, it is within that passion that your ministry will be most effective.

My mother's passion is in the kitchen. She only recently found out that that was also her ministry. My parents carried a lifetime burden to establish a German-oriented church in a major city. For years they tried to give Bible studies and build that church in traditional ways, only to see it dwindle down to around twenty members. But sometime in the last decade something happened in that church. Among other things, my parents stopped trying to be what they were not and concentrated on the gift of hospitality that God had given them all along.

I came home from Andrews one day, walked in the door, and my mother said, "I'd like you to meet your new brother!" He was sitting in the living room, bare to the waist, with a gold chain around his neck and a big gold medallion on his chest. This was going to be an interesting brother! I soon learned of his homosexual orientation. He lived next door, and he would come over for hours at a time and watch my mother do the housework. I don't know what the psychological dynamic was, but he absolutely adored my mother as she opened her life to him.

I found out that my mother had also developed a close relationship with some Buddhist girls who were homosexually orientated. Buddhists! I thought to myself,

"What has happened to my conservative Adventist parents?" One Sabbath there were twenty-five young people home for lunch. Twelve were church members, and thirteen were not. All shared the table out in the yard on a summer afternoon. Everyone felt at home. I began to suspect that my parents had also found home—the place where they could be themselves in service for God.

When my parents left that city a few years ago, there were nearly a hundred young people in that church. Many of them made a point to come over to me and say, "We're so sorry your parents are leaving. They're the reason we're in this church." My mother and father deny to this day that they had anything to do with it, but there are powerful results when we reach out to people in the way that the Holy Spirit designed for us personally to do it.

Many people are gifted in the area of giving Bible studies. Although Bible studies did not work well for my parents, I *do* have a gift for them, so the gifts of the Spirit are not hereditary. We serve happiest and we serve best when we serve in harmony with the gifts and passions that God has given each of us. If we are gifted in the area of Bible studies, we will love it and be successful at it. People will sense that we are making a difference. My parents discovered their unique ministry late in life, and when they did they began reaching a class of people that you or I might never reach.

Nothing will "energize the laity" as much as discovering God's unique plan for each person's life and outreach. No pastor can reach the secular community by himself or herself. It takes an army of people working under the empowerment of the Spirit. When a church activates the energy of the Spirit, the variety of ministries that will emerge is amazing. When people serve God where they don't fit, they go through life unfulfilled and with little success in evangelism. But when they serve at the center of their passion, life becomes the greatest thing on earth. There is no substitute for knowing that you are where God wants you to be and that you're doing what God wants you to do.

I speak from personal experience. I genuinely believe that I am currently placed where God wants me to be, to do what He wants me to do. I do not feel that I am doing the job as well as I could; I have so much to learn and so much growing to do. But various providences over the years make it clear that I should not seek fulfillment elsewhere. And it is hard to top the feeling that comes when you know that you are where God wants you to be and that you're doing what God wants you to do.

A spirit-driven multiplicity of ministries is the perfect complement to the incredible diversity of the Information Age. Secular people are best reached one-on-one through personal interaction. Therefore, it is better to have a hundred ministers than just one. If there are a hundred members in a church, there can be a hundred ministers if the church catches this vision.

Workplace evangelism

One reality of the current situation is the fact that we have moved from the Industrial Age into the Communication Age. This change in the way people think, work, and do business has serious implications for our attempts to reach out to the secular world. I believe that in coming years the best place for evangelism is going to be the workplace. It is in the workplace that more Seventh-day Adventists come in contact with secular people than anywhere else. But many opportunities are lost because the outreach possibilities of the workplace are either misused or go unnoticed. We must not allow misguided or unethical attempts to evangelize the workplace to steer us away from our best opportunity.

One of the best ways to reach secular people in the workplace is through excellence in work performance. Noteworthy excellence impresses secular people that a person has something special going for him or her. This is related to the attractiveness that was mentioned at the close of Part Two. Let me illustrate the powerful impact of excellence on corporate attitudes with a story that occurred in the School of Technology at Andrews University.

There is a firm in Chicago called AGS&R that is considered one of the top two or three multi-image operations in the United States. The Andrews University media-tech department likes to take students to see AGS&R's operation so they can better understand what that kind of life is like. At one of these meetings a student asked the company president a question. "I'm a Seventh-day Adventist, and that means I don't work from Friday night to Saturday night," he said. "If I wanted a job in your company, would that be a problem?"

The president replied, "Yes, that would be a problem because when projects are due around here, we have to work around the clock and on weekends in order to meet deadlines. If you had that kind of restriction, we wouldn't hire you."

Well, that was a real deflator to these young people, who were soon to be seeking jobs in the marketplace. But they stuck with their program anyway. Not long after that, Andrews paid fees to enter a number of student multi-image projects at a festival in Chicago. When the program came out, the teacher discovered to his dismay that all the presentations were scheduled on Sabbath. Since many of these presentations had been shown on Sabbath at the General Conference and in other church settings, the teacher spent some time wrestling with his conscience, but he came to the conclusion that even though these presentations might be appropriate in a Sabbath context, the audience was not going to be in a Sabbath mood. Somehow he felt this was not the thing to do. So he went to the head of that festival and said, "I'm sorry, we cannot allow these things to be shown on Saturday. They have to be moved to another time."

The organizer of the festival said, "I'm sorry. The program's made out, and the way it is, is the way it is."

The teacher replied, "Well, if that's the case, give me the programs. You can keep our money, but we won't be there."

"Oh, let's not be rash about this. Let me see what I can do."

When the time came, all of the Andrews programs were rescheduled for Sunday, and they won festival awards. When the festival was over, the organizer came up to the teacher and said, "I want you to know something. We understand why you took the stand that you did. We really do understand your convictions."

What was he saying? He was saying, "There's something special about you people. Your work is the best. Evidently your convictions must have something to do with that."

Not long after that, a graduating Andrews student went down to AGS&R and said, "I'm from Andrews University. I'm a Seventh-day Adventist. I don't work from Friday night till Saturday night, and I'd like a job here."

The personnel director looked him in the eye and said, "You're hired."

The student said, "What do you mean, I'm hired?"

The personnel director said, "You're hired."

The student again asked why.

"For a very simple reason. You guys are the best."

"Well, what about the Saturday restriction?"

The personnel director responded, "We can't mess with that. There's something about you people that's different, that provides a special excellence in your work. If we were to make you compromise your convictions, you probably wouldn't be any good."

Now, is that a witness? Is that being the salt of the earth? I call that workplace evangelism. It may be different from anything we ever called evangelism before. But the workplace is becoming the best place to make a difference for Christ in the secular environment.

You would be amazed at the hundreds of Adventists who work in the Federal office buildings in Washington, D.C. Several have even reached some of the highest levels. It is tragic that so many are misunderstood in their own churches and do not receive the encouragement and support that would enable them to salt this whole country! A few years back, however, an idea was born that could revolutionize the outreach of this church, making Federal office buildings centers of Adventist influence!

The first step was to find all the Adventists who worked in a particular office building and encourage them to take one lunch a week together. Now this could be frightening from an administrative perspective. You might bring together six Adventists from six different churches in three or four different conferences. But these groups all had one thing in common. They were all interested in the same area of the government's operation. Their work often gave them more in common with each other than they had with their neighbors or the members of their local church! By getting together once a week for lunch, they could talk about what it means to be an Adventist in the Department of Housing and Urban Development, for example. What contribution can the faith make to the needs and concerns that energize the work in that department?

From time to time the groups invited Adventist speakers with specialized expertise to address such concerns and opened the meetings up to their workmates. "Hey, we're going to have this lunch meeting to discuss this issue that's been troubling our department." Since the government encourages and provides space for such informal, work-related get-togethers, the possibilities are enormous.

If the workplace is the best place for evangelism, then I would suggest that we need Seventh-day Adventists everywhere in the workplace. "Go ye into all the world" should not be limited to specialized moments for outreach. Our occupations are part of the world also. Christ longs to reach people in the workplace through Adventist Christians who are fully devoted to Him. The possibilities are especially large in media, education, journalism, and the arts because these are the occupations that influence more people than any others. Such opportunities offer enlarged spheres of influence. I must repeat, however, that such outreach is not for everybody. It should never be undertaken without a full awareness of the dangers discussed in Part Two.

Clifton Davis was a very special student at the Seminary. It was clear that he had the capacity to make a major impact in the secular world if he could find the right niche. I was concerned that the pastorate might not be the place for his unique gifts. There are many, many successful black evangelists in North America. Clifton would clearly have been successful as an evangelist in the fortress and crusade model. There is nothing wrong with that mode. It has a continuing role to play in our outreach. But I had never met a person with Clifton's level of ability to relate to the secular mind. So for three or four months, I felt a burden from the Lord to challenge him to an outreach more along the lines of the salt model. I had no specific idea in mind, and I never quite got the opportunity to share it with him.

Finally one day I saw him in the hall, and I said, "Clifton, I need to see you in my office; there's something I need to talk to you about."

He said, "That's interesting. There's something I want to talk to you about." When he arrived at my office, he said,

"What did you want to talk to me about?"

I said, "Well, you tell me first what you wanted to tell me."

He replied, "I got a call last week from Hollywood. They want to revive my old show and modify it a little bit to where I become pastor of a local church and play that on the show."

I said, "Well, what about the Sabbath?"

"I told the producer that, and he said, 'What's the Sabbath?'

"So I said, 'What do ya mean, what's the Sabbath? You ought to know, you're Jewish! Don't you remember, from Friday night sundown to Saturday night sundown?'

" 'Oh,' he said, 'I had no idea you guys were into that!' "

The producer said that because Clifton is an African-American, and he figured the Sabbath was only for Jews.

"Maybe some of us are keeping it because you don't," Clifton told him. "In any case, I would want Sabbaths off."

The producer said, "Actors don't get that kind of stuff."

"If you want me on the show, I get Sabbath off."

"Well, I'll see what I can do."

He called Clifton back a day later and said, "You've got the Sabbath."

Clifton then said, "One more thing; I want some control over the script. I don't intend to do just anything someone might think up."

The producer protested, "Actors never get control of the script. That's unheard of."

"Then I'm not on the show."

" 'Well, I'll see what I can do.' "

Clifton told me that he had been given significant control over the script through a board of pastors who would examine each script before it would be passed. Things were sounding quite interesting.

I then said, "If you take that route, it would be kind of nice for you to still have some kind of connection with the

Adventist pastorate."

"You're not going to believe this," he said. "Loma Linda University Church just called me up and said they'd like me to be half-time pastor and half-time in Hollywood!"

I don't know how you relate to that, but to me it sounded too much like the hand of God when you put it all together. There have been things on Clifton's show that bother me and other Adventists. But the show was not designed to satisfy an Adventist audience. What Clifton did has to be understood in the light of the entire setting of what this book is all about. I believe in zero-based evangelism. That means that we try almost anything once, and if it doesn't work, try something else. I believe this attitude to be in harmony with counsel that has guided us as a church for years:

> Men are needed who pray to God for wisdom, and who, under the guidance of God, can put new life into the old methods of labor and can invent new plans and new methods of awakening the interest of church members and reaching the men and women of the world (*Evangelism*, 105).
>
> Means will be devised to reach hearts. Some of the methods used in this work will be different from the methods used in the work in the past; but let no one, because of this, block the way by criticism (*Advent Review and Sabbath Herald*, 30 September 1902).

Clifton's presence in Hollywood has made a difference. Hollywood is a unique people-group. You certainly don't reach them from the outside. The place is so insulated that Hollywood actors tend to marry only other Hollywood actors. The only way to reach these people is from inside. And as I talked to Clifton, I became more and more convinced that God had something special in mind here.

Remembering how God used Esther helps me to understand that God has bigger ideas and plans than we do. Not only has Clifton been able to share Christ with some major public names, but I have noticed two changes in Hollywood since his arrival. First, Christians are being portrayed in a more positive light than used to be the case. In the past, Christians made it on television only as Bible-thumping bigots or hypocrites hiding secret vices. Today, Christians are occasionally portrayed as normal people who struggle with significant issues in life. And second, I've noticed more and more actors and athletes who are willing to admit to a relationship with Jesus Christ. This is what salt ministry is all about—influencing the larger society in behalf of the kingdom of God.

But no secular outreach is more dangerous to spirituality than Hollywood. So I warned Clifton along the lines of Part Two of this book. "You must listen to me, Clifton. What you're doing is going to be the most dangerous thing you've ever tried to do since you became a Christian. You're going back into a setting in which you were once an entirely different person. And frankly, the odds are pretty strong that, without special safeguards, you're going to lose your way."

I continued, "What you need is a person who knows you better than you know yourself, who will watch you and observe you and stay close to you. And you must be open and honest with this friend. You need to make a contract with your friend that if the day ever comes when he says, 'Clifton, you're losing it,' you'll quit Hollywood on the spot and walk away. If you don't do this, I can't advise you to go."

He said, "I know a person like that, and I will do that."

The day may come when Clifton decides it was a mistake. If you don't agree with what he is doing, I respect that and he respects it. But instead of writing a hate-filled letter, let me suggest something more effective. Pray for him. He needs your encouragement and your prayers.

And so do many others in similar positions. If the workplace is becoming the best place for evangelism, it will at times be necessary to take some risks. "Preachers" who are not daily energized by the disciplines of the Spirit will drift until they become "castaways," to use Paul's language in 1 Corinthians 9. We need to spiritually hold up the hands of those taking such risks for Christ. It is not for everybody, but if God should bring you to a special place of influence, you can know that you are there for a specific purpose and that you will have the opportunity to exalt God in a unique way.

12

Outreach Through Worship

One of the great "hot potatoes" in the Adventist Church today is the subject of worship. That must not prevent us, however, from noting the centrality of worship style to the impact that Adventism makes or does not make in a secular world. I have already suggested that the typical Adventist worship service tends to turn off secular people. As secular people begin to come to an Adventist church, are there ways we can make them feel more at home?

It is possible that the two models of ministry found in Matthew 5:13-16 should be expanded to a third. While the first two models illustrate the two major ways individuals can involve themselves in gospel outreach, there is a third way that involves the group as a whole. The fortress city of Matthew 5:14 is associated with the metaphor of a bright and shining light that cannot be hidden. This suggests that the church as a corporate whole, when it enjoys the fullness of the abundant life and the mutual love that is available in Christ, exerts a powerful attraction upon those who are outside. A truly biblical community will draw people in by its very existence.

While public evangelism often succeeds in increasing baptisms, it does not always result in sustained church growth. One reason for this is that the people didn't join a

Saturday-morning church. They joined a church that meets five nights a week, uses lots of visual aids, and has exciting music by professionals or with taped accompaniment. They are then expected to settle for once a week, few visual aids if any, and a piano or organ played with a minimum of enthusiasm. A little reflection indicates that the quality of Sabbath worship is crucial to sustaining church growth, not just among secular people, but in general.

Many Adventist churches, therefore, are now finding that a relevant and vibrant worship service has a powerful, word-of-mouth drawing power upon the unchurched. Those who have fallen away from church attendance because the worship service seemed boring, manipulative, and out of touch with their lives are often open to giving church another chance when the worship service is interesting and speaks powerfully to contemporary issues.

Part of this worship renewal includes a use of contemporary language and harmonic idioms. While this has appeared threatening to some, history teaches us that revivals of faith are usually accompanied by revivals of Christian song-writing. The need for fresh melodies, styles, and lyrics lies in the fact that faith must touch base with real life if it is to become the everyday experience that is needed to overcome secular drift. Contemporary secular songs, though often presenting messages that are contrary to the gospel, nevertheless express deeply the struggles of life in today's world. When Christian music demonstrates an awareness of those contemporary struggles, it has a powerful influence in behalf of the gospel's solutions to those struggles. Thus, it is not surprising that many of the great hymns of the past utilized contemporary lyrics and melodies to bring Christianity home in a relevant way. We must not be afraid to be as bold as the hymnwriters of the past.

Before I continue, let me explain that I too once feared

that contemporary music might lead us in a dangerous direction. I have now changed my mind. Let me explain how it happened. Some time ago our home church faced a lengthy period of time without a pastor. As part of its worship plan the church invited the youth (ages fourteen to twenty-two) to present a youth worship service on a monthly basis. This included contemporary praise songs (no drums, very low key), a dramatic sketch illustrating the theme of the sermon, and a sermon that spoke directly to contemporary issues. A number of exciting things happened almost overnight. The youth group for the first time felt that it was a valued and accepted part of the church. Young people got excited about the chance to contribute. Not only did the youth group grow rapidly, but they brought parents and friends, and soon the attendance at our church had more than doubled. No parking was available after 9:20 a.m.!

What impressed me most, however, was what happened to my own children. Up until then they had expressed the usual disinterest in everything that happened in the church service with the exception of the children's story. But during the youth services, their eyes and ears were entirely up front. I knew this not only from the looks on their faces and the unused Magna-Doodles lying on the pew, but from what happened the rest of the week. All week long I could hear them singing the songs that they had heard and seen on the screen during the worship service. But even more impressive is the fact that I often heard the three-year-old and the four-year-old exchanging one-liners from the sermon during the course of the week! Somehow the use of contemporary songs and the visual medium of the skit communicated to children that the sermon was also relevant to them. Somehow, in a subtle way that I do not understand, my children perceived that worship was worth their time and energy.

Please keep in mind that we do not even have a television set in our house, so our children are not "jaded" by hours of bleary-eyed saturation in the secular world.

That's when I realized that none of us are fully insulated from contemporary life. Though we may shun the television and radio, we are influenced nevertheless. When you call a bank, a store, or the credit-card company, they put you on hold, and guess what comes over the phone! When you go to the grocery store or the shopping mall to obtain items necessary for life, what kind of music comes over the PA system? It is impossible to live totally in our own world. When worship fails to speak to the world we live in, it is easy to live a double life. One is the life that we live when we are in church or associating with fellow Christians. The other is the life we live as we work and play. Such a compartmentalized life will neither save us from secular drift nor attract secular people to our faith.

Some time after the "youth experience" in our church I visited a major city in a third-world country. In that city were two pastors. One pastored a "celebration" church, and the other pastored an "anti-celebration" church. It was hoped that a joint worship service of the churches might help to build relationships and understanding. I stayed at the home of the "anti-celebration" pastor. An interesting thing happened at sundown on Friday. The television and the VCR were turned on, and throughout the Sabbath hours contemporary Christian music videos from Adventist groups played in endless cycle. Much of the music was of a racier variety than that used at the "celebration" church in town. I was stunned. I said to the conference official who had brought me to that city, "This man opposes using this kind of music at the eleven-o'clock hour but enjoys it the rest of the week. Do you realize what this does? It means that worship is the one hour of the week that is totally cut off from the rest of his experience. The Sabbath-morning worship service is almost guaranteed not to speak to what matters most in his day-to-day life." I say this, not to be critical of a very godly pastor, but to illustrate how easily worship becomes isolated from our everyday experience. Rather than being the driving force behind our outreach for God, it's an obligation to be performed.

I have learned one more thing from my church's short-lived experiment with contemporary Christianity. The youth services are now a thing of the past in our little church. The attendance has dropped back to previous levels. The youth have settled back into their isolation. My children no longer pay attention to the worship service. Things are back to normal! I have learned that, as a group, change is a very wrenching experience for church people, even when the results are dramatic. We must not forget that many people do appreciate a more traditional worship style. Many of the great hymns of the church still speak powerfully. There is nothing inherently wrong with the traditional service. If it is working well where you are, don't throw it out! Not only do many people prefer the traditional style, but maintaining it has become a matter of conscience for them. It is a terrible thing to force such people to go against their conscience.

I have, therefore, concluded from my own experience, and that of others I have worked with, that it is usually unwise to try to make large changes in the worship style of a local church, even though change may be a positive thing for many. Too many souls are troubled, too many hearts are broken. This world has enough tears already! And it hardly seems fair to take a church that has functioned in one place for decades and "tear it away" from those who have given their lives to it. I plead that those who have a passion for reaching the secular mind have compassion on those who do not. The fortress model is not a sin. It is just a different model of ministry! Coercion and force are tools of Satan, even when exerted in a good cause. It is a terrible thing to be forced to go against one's conscience.

If worship style is to be a central component of outreach to a secular world, it may be better to start a fresh congregation that is dedicated to outreach on a contemporary basis. Those who prefer a more traditional style can continue to go where that style remains in force. Just as individuals have unique gifts that can be applied to God's work, so churches may also be gifted to carry out tasks that other churches could not accomplish. I must, therefore, plead with those who prefer the traditional idiom not to burden the lives of those who bravely strive to raise up new churches. Do not trouble them with bitter and endless criticism. I realize that such "praise churches" will gain some of the best and brightest from other Adventist churches, and thus cannot go unnoticed. But this will be a wondrous opportunity to speak the most difficult, yet the greatest words ever spoken by a sinner: "He must increase, but I must decrease" (John 3:30, KJV). There is room in our church for more than one model of worship, just as there is room for more than one model of ministry.

In many geographical areas of this country, however, there are hardly enough Adventists in a community to keep one church afloat, much less two. In such circumstances it makes little sense to orient an entire church, kicking and screaming, into targeting exclusively the classes of people who are most difficult to reach, especially when such targeting involves spiritual risk. The best that one could hope for from the worship service in such a setting is that the service would at least not be hostile to a secular seeker. The goal would be to design a church service that can, on the one hand, meet the needs of traditional Adventists, while at the same time providing a more "user-friendly" environment for secular people. In the following I offer six suggestions that could be introduced into any Seventh-day Adventist church without a board action. None of these suggestions compromise the basics that are vital to the spiritual health of more traditional people in Adventist congregations; yet, if followed, they would make the worship service more inviting and attractive to secular people.

First, it helps a great deal to use everyday language—the language that is understood on the street—in all parts of the worship service, rather than the in-house lingo of Adventism. We mentioned this already in the chapter entitled "Cutting-Edge People." The use of common, everyday language is important for at least two reasons. One reason was mentioned in Part One, where we noticed that God has always gone out of His way to communicate with human beings in their contemporary culture and idiom. While everyday language may at times seem a limited tool for expressing the realities of the spiritual realm, the power with which it can unify the spiritual realm with everyday life makes up for any such limitations. A second reason to use common language is that it expresses caring. When we go out of our way to communicate with people in a way that meets them where they are, it communicates that we care enough to understand where they are coming from. They matter to us. When people know that they matter to other humans, it makes it easier for them to believe that they matter also to God.

Avoiding Adventist jargon will not kill anybody. No one will leave the church if we stop using words like *investment* and *light* in our unique way. This is not a major sacrifice for someone who is accustomed to a more traditional style of worship. It lets people from a variety of backgrounds know that they are welcome. They don't need to learn a new language as an initiation. Where hymns, Scripture readings, or other worship aids are in the obscure language of the past, a short, well-prepared introduction can help people relate to the original setting of the language, and thus they can meaningfully engage with the sentiments expressed. The bottom line here is to make sure that everything we do in the worship service is readily understandable to the secular person who may wander in or be invited by a member.

A second change that will make a major difference in how "user-friendly" a church is to secular people is to make sure that whatever happens on Sabbath morning has high "take-home value." It should be usable on Monday morning. How many Seventh-day Adventist sermons are worth a dime on the street? How often do our sermons have any impact on the way we really live? Are we just spending excess time? I tremble to think that if a thousand people attend a church service and nothing significant happens for an hour, you've wasted half a work-year of life. Preaching needs to have high take-home value. People need to be hearing something that they can apply on Monday, Tuesday, and Wednesday mornings. And you can do that without compromising the faith one iota.

> Ministers should not preach sermon after sermon on doctrinal subjects alone. Practical godliness should find a place in every discourse (*Advent Review and Sabbath Herald*, 23 April 1908).

> In laboring in a new field, do not think it your duty to say at once to the people, We are Seventh-day Adventists; we believe that the seventh day is the Sabbath; we believe in the non-immortality of the soul. This would often erect a formidable barrier between you and those you wish to reach. Speak to them, as you have opportunity, upon points of doctrine on which you can agree. Dwell on the necessity of practical godliness. Give them evidence that

> you are a Christian, desiring peace, and that you love their souls. Let them see that you are conscientious. Thus you will gain their confidence; and there will be time enough for doctrines. Let the heart be won, the soil prepared, and then sow the seed, presenting in love the truth as it is in Jesus (*Gospel Workers*, 119, 120).

While Ellen White probably had geographical new fields in mind when she wrote this counsel, the secular environment certainly qualifies as a "new field" for us at this time. Few secular people have heard of us, and few of them know what we believe. For such individuals, a demonstration of practical, living Christianity will be an attractive force that will invite them to inquire further into godliness. I have found that when I teach people how to live, I offend no one, but develop all kinds of interest in the study of the Scriptures and the overcoming of sin in the life. This counsel should be so obvious that one wonders why practical godliness does not ring from every Adventist pulpit every Sabbath. The answer may lie in a chilling statement that lays open the grounds why my own preaching has often been ineffective:

> It is a sad fact that the reason why many dwell so much on theory and so little on practical godliness is that Christ is not abiding in their hearts. They do not have a living connection with God (*Testimonies for the Church*, 4:395, 396).

We will become effective in presenting how a Christian copes with Monday morning when we ourselves have wrestled honestly with the issues people face at home, in the neighborhood, and on the job. When we ourselves know how to walk with God every day of the week, we will be able to teach others to do the same. The churches that are making the greatest impact in the secular world today are emphasizing practical Christianity. (Other important Ellen White statements on practical godliness are: *Gospel Workers*, 158, 159; *Testimonies* 3:237; *Testimonies* 5:158, 539).

A third area that makes a big difference with secular people is a concern for excellence, for quality in everything that we do as a church. Too often Adventist churches look shabby in the extreme. The choice of participants and the content of the worship service is clearly an afterthought. The sermon and the special music seem thrown together at the last minute. Some Adventists may tolerate shabbiness, but secular people consider shabbiness to be an insult both to their intelligence and to their sense of stewardship of time.

I think we can learn a great deal on this point from The Disney Corporation. A major reason for Disney's success is that it insists on excellence in every detail of its parks. You will never see a garbage dumpster around the corner of a building in a Disney park. They do not want a single thing to detract from the visitor's experience. There is excellence in the music, excellence in the decor, excellence in every detail. The same is generally true of television. While the content may be contrary to the gospel, it is usually served up with supreme care. Hours of work go into every minute. This is particularly true in the case of commercials. Multiplied hours and huge numbers of dollars are spent to make a single minute as productive as possible in its impact on the viewer.

Although we demand quality in the products we buy, the motels we stay in, and the programming we enjoy, we somehow expect a secular person to enjoy a halfhearted sermon and a thoroughly butchered song. But instead of enjoyment, that person will report to his or her friends on

Monday morning, "You should have seen the sorry excuse for a church service I saw this weekend. There was a singer there who must have had her throat removed in an operation, it was so bad. And the pastor had no idea what he was talking about. He was unbelievable."

"Oh, what church was that?"

All it takes is one report like that, and you have destroyed the church's credibility with not one, but five or six, maybe even ten people.

Is excellence that difficult? Is the worship service so unimportant that it doesn't matter? Isn't worshiping God worth the very best that we can offer, whether we're preaching, singing, or praying? We have come to a place in earth's history where we need to be the best that we can be for God. Less than the best isn't good enough anymore.

In saying this I must confess that as a pastor I had much too flippant an attitude toward those parts of the worship service that I didn't "star" in personally. The music, the Scripture, the prayer, and even the announcements are worthy of careful planning and skilled execution.

Having said this, I would like to qualify it just a bit so as not to discourage the many small churches that may seem devoid of world-class talent. On the subject of excellence, it may be helpful to make some distinction between mistakes of enthusiasm and mistakes of carelessness. What I am talking about here are mistakes of carelessness and neglect. Just as secular people are forgiving about social mistakes if one is genuine and open, they can also tell the difference between sincere effort and carelessness or between enthusiasm and phoniness.

One of the best ways to enhance excellence in any operation is to evaluate and critique on a regular basis. As threatening as evaluation may be, if we are serious about excellence, we need to constantly get feedback regarding the quality of our efforts for God. The ministries and services of a church should constantly be measured in relation to the Word of God and the needs of the people being served. No one should consider himself exempt, not even the pastor. I learn much more from people who disagree with me, because they will often tell me to my face things that my friends may not have the courage to express. The evaluation process is always painful, but it results in a much more effective ministry.

Even the best of sermons can be improved upon. Quite recently I preached a sermon at a large church in an institutional setting that seemed to have a significant impact on a lot of people. Small clusters of people gathered spontaneously all over the campus that afternoon to discuss the implications of the sermon for their lives. I felt good that God had used me to make a difference. But in the receiving line a man came up to me with disappointment written all over his face. He had difficulty believing that a detail in my sermon was factual as I had inferred. That "lie" had ruined the whole sermon for him.

I slipped immediately into a defensive mode. I indicated that I could give names and dates and places to verify every detail. He just shook his head and said, "I'm sorry, I just can't believe it happened that way, I'm sorry." He left unreconciled. The story I had told was in fact true. I felt justifiably angry that my integrity had been challenged by a stranger. Upon reflection, however, I realized that ministers are not exempt from the temptation to exaggerate and embellish stories from time to time. Like my challenger, I, too, find that the practice of exaggeration can detract from an otherwise excellent message. I realized in retrospect that although the story I had told was factually accurate, it *was* stranger than fiction. And if even one person (and for every one who confronts, a dozen may keep silence) lost the blessing of the sermon because he questioned that detail, the sermon would be better off without it. It was not, in any case, crucial to my main point. I hope that I can meet this man again someday and thank him for making me a better preacher.

A fourth area that can make a difference is directly related to the reality of the media. Worship needs to be more visual and attention grabbing than before. What do people do with those little radar guns that turn all the channels on the TV? It drives me nuts. They sit there—click, watch for five seconds; click, on to the next channel; click, on to the next channel, ranging through. What are they doing? Looking for something worth spending time on. How long do they take to decide? Five or ten seconds per channel at the most.

Preacher, if you never thought about this before, fasten your seat belt. The kind of people we are talking about here, many of whom sit in your pews, will decide after ten seconds whether your sermon is worth listening to, because they have been trained to make that kind of decision! Thus, the very first sentence becomes "do or die." Speakers these days must grab people right at the start and then keep them listening throughout. People's attention cannot be taken for granted anymore.

Grabbing attention is in harmony with the example of Christ, who had a fascinating way of asking those little rhetorical questions like, "Which of these two sons really obeyed his father?" In that society, a story and a question like that turned the temple court into an E. F. Hutton seminar. Today, we may only have five or ten seconds to make a case for people to listen to the sermon.

Music, if it is done well, can enhance the attention quotient of a worship service. Equally effective is the use of visual aids in communication, such as drama. While the word *drama* may frighten some Adventists, we make powerful use of drama in nearly every Adventist church on Sabbath morning. We call it the children's story. And guess who gets the most out of the children's story? The two-year-olds usually ignore it. The children's story is there for the adults! They would be upset if you didn't have one.

You can't fool me. I start dramatizing a Bible story for the kids and then peek out of the corner of my eye. All the adults are leaning forward with their eyes as big as saucers. They don't want to miss anything. So I really lay it on thick. I lie down, I snore, I stand on my head (well, almost!), all kinds of things. And if the kids love it, the adults love it even more. Some of these same adults would be upset if we had a drama or showed a video. Then I get into the pulpit and watch them settling down for their snooze!

Case closed.

Drama brings spiritual lessons home with contemporary power in a way that few things can.

If the people in your church are dead set against drama, use the children's story instead. Coordinate it with the sermon, the hymns, and the Scripture reading; make the whole service one of a piece. Let the children's story set the tone for the sermon. Let it raise a question or a problem. By the time the pastor gets up to speak, people are already thinking, "Well, how are we going to solve this problem?" Let the children's story be longer and the sermon a little shorter, but build the two together, and the whole service will have more zip.

We are all accustomed to drama in one form or another, so the word itself should not turn us off. In this day and age, where people have grown up with television, we certainly accomplish little if we put them to sleep. The small changes recommended here need not offend those of a more traditional bent. It certainly does not help to go into a church with a heavy hand and say, "We're going to start introducing drama into this church." You will have a fight on your hands. Just make the children's story more creative and more integrated with the whole service, and you'll accomplish the same result without the fuss.

The fifth matter that is critical to worship renewal is strong spiritual tone. Truth is not enough to keep people in church today. Most backsliders still believe the truth. My wife's mother, for example, spent twenty-five years out of the church, yet she could argue any Baptist under the table over the Sabbath! Truth is not enough to keep people anymore. It must be combined with spiritual life. People need to experience a living God. When secular people decide to come to church, it is because they sense that the living God is present there. Secular people are drawn to churches where the people know God and know how to teach others to know God.

There is nothing un-Adventist about spirituality; there is nothing heretical about prayer and Bible study. Right now in our church of about a hundred members, there are three prayer groups meeting every week. There is increasing interest in our denomination in family devotions, prayer, and spiritual life in the church. The concepts discussed in Part Two of this book are one way to approach the issue of spirituality in the church.

When secular people start seeking faith, they are looking for evidence that God is real and that other people experience Him. A church made up of people who know God and who know how to teach others how to know Him will draw secular people in like a magnet. Everything that is done, whether it is the sermon, the special music, or the prayer, needs to be driven by the spiritual vitality of those who participate. Secular people are not easily fooled. If the spiritual life of the church is phony, it will fool no one, certainly not its own youth.

This brings us to the sixth area of potential improvement in Adventist worship, and probably the most important one. People today are crying out for examples of genuine, authentic Christianity; or to use street terms, being real.

Not long ago I was sitting at dinner with a number of leading thinkers in the Adventist Church. At one point in the conversation, they turned to me and said, "Jon, what do you think is the greatest need of the Adventist Church right now?" Almost without thinking I responded, "To stop living a lie!"

Well, that stopped the discussion right in its tracks, but the more I thought about my casual reply, the more compelling it became. So often in Adventist churches, people are just going through the motions, playing church. Why do you go to church? Do you go because your mother did? Or because you want your children to get a religious education? Or do you go because . . . just because you go? Is churchgoing just a game we play, and once it's out of the way we can have fun the rest of the week? Secular people seem to have a sixth sense about who is genuine and who is not. They can smell phony Christians a mile away.

What does it mean to be genuine and authentic? Authenticity is when the inside is in harmony with the outside. Living a lie is where the inside and the outside are two different things. It was reported to me that at a meeting of Christian leaders the discussion became so hot the participants began shouting back and forth, and some swear words were used. A couple of ministers even threatened each other physically. Suddenly, at seven-thirty that evening, a knock came on the door, and someone entered and said, "Don't you know what time it is? The people are here for the prayer meeting." The fellow who had been right at the center of the fight walked out in front of the assembly and said, "Isn't it good when brethren dwell together in unity? Isn't it good to be together with the people of God tonight?"

If I had been there, it would have made me ill. Why did he do it? Was it to protect his image as a Christian leader? The reality is that the phony is usually the last person to know that everyone knows he or she is a phony.

What would be true Christian genuineness in that situation? To act as if nothing had happened would be to live a lie. Should the leader have come out swearing instead? No, that would not be Christian either. I would hope that between the office and the pulpit he might have gotten the realization that something was dreadfully wrong. It would be genuine to come up before the people and say, "You know, we've just had a meeting backstage. And frankly, some of us didn't behave much like Christ. I'm really not worthy to stand up here and run this meeting. But I know that in Christ there is a way to be forgiven and a way to change. First of all, I need to apologize to these brethren over here. And second, we all need to kneel down so that *you* can pray for *us*, because we need it desperately." That would be genuine. And secular people would find that kind of religion much more attractive than one that is always sweetly smiling when it's not really for real.

I remember a student who enjoyed expressing his irritation at "them"—the administrators of the Adventist Church. Right and wrong seem so much easier to determine when you are not at the center of the decision-making processes. Since he was a fun-loving, unorthodox person, he certainly did not fit the typical mold of Adventist administration. Nevertheless, because of his considerable administrative and people skills, I warned him that he was in real danger of becoming one of "them" some day. Thus it was with some amusement and no little excitement that I greeted the news some time later that he had indeed become one of "them." He had been elected to an administrative post. Would he maintain the carefree and independent spirit so natural to his personality, or would he try to fit into the mold?

Some years later we were assigned to the same church committee. At break time I moved across the room to greet him with a high five and a, "Hey, man, how's it going?" He stood up regally in his three-piece suit, put out his hand formally, and said in a measured voice, "Hello, Jon, so nice to see you again." He had become one of "them"! He was now playing the role of his new position, a role so unlike his previous demeanor. I found myself quite disheartened by the encounter. Christianity must be more than just an image that we project. (To tell the rest of the story, I am glad to report that he has since relaxed into his new duties and become much more human again!)

The essence of Christian authenticity is to "be what you are." This does not mean that if you feel like the devil you should also act like the devil. Any secular person can be authentic in that way. Christian authenticity is more challenging. "Being what you are" brings a Christian face to face with the reality that what we are and what we ought to be are two different things. But for the authentic Christian there is only one possible course of action. If what you are isn't right, you need to go to the Lord, confess where you are, and invite His involvement in your life to transform you into a "who you are in Christ."

To serve Him as effectively as possible means diet; it means devotional life; it means learning to remold some of our attitudes and personality traits, not in order to be saved, but for Christ's sake, and for the sake of lost people.

The matter lies very close to home for me. When I started out in the ministry, I used to get a splitting headache every Sabbath. It was very frustrating, because on the very day that I needed to be at my best for God, I was feeling my worst. A couple of years later it finally dawned on me (some people are slow learners) that the reason for the Sabbath headaches was that I was trying to be someone I was not in front of the people. I was playing a role. I was being what I thought people wanted me to be rather than what I truly ought to be in Christ. God helped me finally to understand that He wanted me to be myself for Him, not Billy Graham or H. M. S. Richards or Roland Hegstad. Just be Jon Paulien for Christ. What a relief! What a blessing! I know from sharing this with Adventists around the world that the reality of "Sabbath headaches" is more widespread than I would like to think.

The most effective path to true authenticity is to cultivate genuineness each day in a devotional encounter with God. Christ can help you to see yourself as others see you. In Christ it is possible to learn how to be yourself. Certainly you cannot be transparent with people if you are not transparent with God. Have you ever lied to God in prayer? "Dear Lord, I love You so much," when in the back of your mind you are thinking, "Boy, I'd like to punch You right in the nose." Yet God prefers that we tell it like it is in prayer. Jesus certainly did. "Why have You forsaken Me?" If Jesus could be honest with God, it cannot be a sin for us! The Lord wants to hear our deepest needs, our deepest feelings—yes, even our anger. Anything but trying to fool Him with sweet-talking words that mean nothing.

Do you know why confession and repentance are essential to salvation? Because confession and repentance are simply acknowledging the truth about ourselves. Not to confess and not to repent is to live a lie before the world. It is to be more concerned with one's image than with reality. Do you remember that Jesus said something about dirty cups with a shiny exterior? We are all dirty cups. But there is one thing uglier than a dirty cup, and that is a dirty cup that goes around telling everyone how clean it is. In the light of the cross, the only authentic existence is to live in continual and transparent repentance.

But what if you don't *feel* repentant? What if, like me, you were gifted with the temperament that knows and uses all the words in every language except the two that say, "I'm sorry"? People like me need help in order to discover the truth about ourselves. What I am about to share with you, therefore, derives from the deepest and most vulnerable facets of my personality.

I have learned as a biblical scholar how easy it is to make the Bible say whatever you want it to say. One's interpretation often arises out of the need to protect one's personal failings and shortcomings from coming to the light of Scripture and the Spirit's gentle persuasion. Our interpretation of Scripture can be made to serve as a wall of denial to protect us from having to acknowledge our sins and weaknesses to God and to others. I have learned that when I sit down to "exegete" Scripture, it must be with the prayer, "Lord, I want the truth, *no matter what the cost*." We are often willing to learn the truth as long as it doesn't cost us anything. But knowing and living the truth can cost us our job, our friends, our family, everything that matters most. It can mean carrying a cross for the rest of our days. So don't pray such a prayer if you don't mean it. I guarantee you, however, that God delights to answer the prayer, "I want the truth, no matter what the cost." He delights to give you the truth. But along with the truth there is a price to pay.

The first time I prayed this prayer was about twelve years ago. I lay face down, in frustration pounding a wooden floor with my fist. The man who had ministered Christ to me now told me in persuasive and logical sincerity that if I truly loved Jesus, I would also need to leave the church I loved. Some of you will not be able to understand why that challenge was so difficult for me at the time. Others have gone through the same experience I did. After much struggle, I opened myself to God and prayed, "Lord, give me the truth, no matter what the cost."

The answer God placed in my mind was crystal clear, although I heard no audible voice. "I understand what you are going through. Remember this, the disciples of Jesus never left Judaism. Luther never left the Catholic Church. Ellen White never left the Methodist Church. All were thrown out. It is My purpose that you should stay in the Adventist Church until you are thrown out. But I have a condition for you. From now on you must not act and speak to protect your job or your social standing. You must tell the truth exactly as you see it without fear or favor. Don't be obnoxious or rebellious or give them some human reason to throw you out. Let it be on the basis that you told the truth, and the truth only. If they throw you out as a result, so be it. That will be My signal to you that I have something better for you."

This message was clearly for me personally. If the Lord gave you a different message at that time, I have no problem with that. To be honest, however, at the time I passed through this experience, I did not think that the Adventist Church could handle the truth. I did not expect to last long. But to my great surprise, my path from that moment on has been only in the direction of greater and greater influence within the church. In spite of what many say these days, my experience has been that the Adventist Church is filled from top to bottom with people who are eager for truth and authenticity. This is as true at the General Conference level as at any other. Although many consider me to now be in a position where I have to "cover my tracks" in order to defend the church, I have seen no reason to deviate from the counsel the Lord gave me twelve years ago, and I have no intention of doing so, as this book will testify. I may be wrong, but I am telling it as I see it, whatever the cost.

Truth telling has not been an easy experience for me. I find myself sabotaged at times at the most inward levels of my being. Natural defense mechanisms threaten my very best intentions. Recently, for example, I tried to analyze why a particular preacher had such a powerful effect on me. It dawned on me after a while that nearly every illustration in his sermons came from personal experience, and that almost all of those illustrations were of his failures and not of his successes. I compared his sermons with my own preaching. I realized that I featured only my successes and not my failures. I was smitten to the core of my being. Another's confession was my road to confession. The truly authentic Christian will be slow to boast and quick to forgive, because such a person will see his own depravity clearly.

As we reach out to the secular people in our communities, we will discover that one of the best ways to find the point of contact in another person is through our own confession of need. People are reluctant to make themselves vulnerable to others. But if we allow ourselves to be vulnerable with them (at the appropriate time and in an appropriate way), they may feel comfortable with sharing their deepest needs and concerns with us.

I have learned, therefore, that I must take my prayer for truth to a deeper level yet. I need more than just biblical truth in order to be effective for God. I need the truth about *myself*. I need to discover when my subconscious defense mechanisms are defeating my very best intentions. The perilous prayer that opens the depths goes something like this: "Lord, I open myself to Your inspection [see Heb. 4:12, 13]. See me as I truly am. Teach me the truth about myself, no matter what the cost. Help me to see myself as You see me." This prayer is a frightening but marvelous opening to the journaling experience. When we open ourselves to God's inspection, He will gently and kindly lead us to things we could never discover any other way. And He will not open to us more than we can handle at the time we pray (see John 16:12).

> The closer you come to Jesus, the more faulty you will appear in your own eyes; for your vision will be clearer, and your imperfections will be seen in broad and distinct contrast to His perfect nature. This is evidence that Satan's delusions have lost their power; that the vivifying influence of the Spirit of God is arousing you.
>
> No deep-seated love for Jesus can dwell in the heart that does not realize its own sinfulness. The soul that is transformed by the grace of Christ will admire His divine character; but if we do not see our own moral deformity, it is unmistakable evidence that we have not had a view of the beauty and excellence of Christ (*Steps to Christ*, 64, 65).

There is yet a deeper level to Christian authenticity. Many of us are so steeped in denial of sin and weakness that we deceive ourselves even in our innermost prayer life. To such people, personal journals can become self-serving accounts of their wisdom and the folly of those around them. There is no substitute, therefore, for the checks and balances that come into our life when we become willing to hear the truth about how others see us. Authentic Christians can usually point to specific people who understand and love them, yet are willing to tell the truth about the quality of their behavior. Accountability to others can enhance our accountability to God.

Such accountability can take various forms. There are three Adventist Christian men in three different parts of the world who play this role in my life. I know that I can call or visit any of them any time. I know that they will tell me to my face whatever I need to hear. They have played a major role in any successes I have had in God's cause. I know of others who found that a small group such as Al-Anon provided the context where they could take off the mask, be real, and get the kind of feedback they needed. In ideal situations, even a Sabbath School class can provide accountability. For those who have few friends and no group to turn to, the only possibility for true accountability may be a personal counseling situation (which should no longer be thought of as a negative option for *any* Christian). Get feedback wherever you can, but get it!

> There are souls perplexed with doubt, burdened with infirmities, weak in faith, and unable to grasp the Unseen; but a friend whom they can see, coming to them in Christ's stead, can be a connecting link to fasten their trembling faith upon Christ (*The Desire of Ages*, 297).

Please allow a momentary digression. I fear that some Adventists may take authenticity as a license to dump on others whatever gossip and negative suspicions they may collect in the course of church life. Some personality types love to "tell it like it is" in the most brutal ways. To all such, I commend the gentleness of Jesus, who said, "I have much more to say to you, but more than you can now bear" (John 16:12). Jesus cares enough about our feelings to wait for the right moment before sharing something that may be hard to bear. And the next verse (John 16:13) makes clear that the Spirit can often communicate what human beings cannot. Authenticity does not require us to tell the whole truth in any and every circumstance. It does require us not to live a lie.

This is, perhaps, the best place in the book to state that while the gospel of justification in the finished work of Christ has not been addressed thus far in this book, it is an assumption that lies in the background of all that has been said here. If we were justified by works rather than by faith, learning the authentic truth about ourselves would destroy us. If we did not have the assurance of salvation in Christ, all the devotional and lifestyle suggestions of the second part of this book would be sounding brass and tinkling cymbals! Understood in Christ, however, the practical suggestions of this book can make a vital difference in people's lives. The main reason why many Adventists seek to avoid reality, I believe, is that they have not clearly understood and appropriated the New Testament gospel.

In conclusion, as I come in contact with ex-Adventists, the number-one excuse for not returning to church is that "they all claim to be so holy, yet they do this and this and that." Such excuses may at times be exaggerated, but if there is one thing above all others that will draw secular people into a church, it is the sense that the people they meet there are living real lives with real struggles and real failures; that they are, in Christ, growing in grace and in love for one another as failing but forgiven human beings. Nothing gives me more courage in faith than to realize that my fellow brothers and sisters struggle with the same things I do and that I can face my problems together with others who care about me. The greatest need of Adventism in the nineties is to make an end of living a lie.

13

How Two Models Can Coexist

What can you do if your local church has no burden for secular people, and there is no possibility of an alternative church setting? If attempts to educate the local leadership on how secular people respond and think have failed, the solution is to form a "subculture" within the church, or to put it another way, to open a door into that church for secular people. If the worship service is not "user-friendly" to secular people, they need to be introduced to another type of church setting first.

This insight first came to me as I was addressing this subject at a conference camp meeting. The conference president became quite excited over the kind of people who were attending the seminar. In particular he mentioned a non-Christian husband who had been resisting the church's attention for years, but when his wife told him about my seminar on meeting the secular mind-set, he eagerly attended. The president had been working with the man for years and was thrilled to see him showing some interest. The next day that husband and his wife came to see me with another couple. The husband said, "I need to talk to you. I appreciate what you have been saying, but I have a problem. I believe in everything your church teaches, but I can't stand the church itself.

What do I do?" By "church" he meant the local congregation. As he spoke to me, the other three nodded their heads approvingly.

Since I run into this all the time, I said, "It seems as if you have a least three people here who understand you. Are there others?"

"Oh, yeah. There are ten to twelve others whom I can relate to pretty well. But the church as a whole—I just can't stand it."

"What you need to do is form a subculture," I said.

"A what-culture?"

My answer to him is my answer to loyal Adventists with the same problem. There are churches where the corporate personality is such that it cannot work effectively with secular people. In such cases, those who carry a burden for lost secular people need to form a subculture within the church.

A subculture is a setting in which a particular class of people who belong to the church or are interested in the church but don't quite fit socially or politically can get the spiritual uplift they need. It's a halfway house, if you wish. A subculture aimed at the secular mind-set would intentionally avoid the minor irritations that drive secular people away from churches. Such a subculture can take many forms. It could be a Sabbath School class, a prayer group, a home Bible-study group, or even a social club.

So I said to these two couples, "You need a subculture, a place where you can have your needs met. If the church service is not meeting your needs, instead of agitating and dividing the church, find a time and a place every week you get together and feed your souls from Scripture.

Ideally, of course, the pastor would be consulted and involved to some degree in each subculture functioning within his church so that unnecessary misunderstandings would not develop.

When I was pastoring in New York City, I had five or six subcultural groups in my church. The motivating principle for one group was family life; another was raising children. In one case we had a group looking into UFOs! Other groups at one time or another included a men's class on how to understand and treat women, a group on personal finances, another on gifts of the Spirit, and several studying various books of the Bible. The main purpose of these subcultures was getting people who had common interests together so that their spiritual and social needs could be met in a way that was rarely possible in the setting of the whole body. In my church the makeup of these subcultures tended to be half members and half secular people. And the members who attended these groups were usually the fringe people who had never been fully at home in the larger church. They ate up these subcultures with joy. Some tried to attend them all! And they rejoiced at bonds they were developing with otherwise unchurched people.

By means of these subcultures, we were able to provide a door to the church for people who wouldn't have felt at home in the church otherwise. Sometimes these secular people would come for two or three years and indicate no further interest in the church. I waited, because I knew that visiting too soon could be a problem for them. Then all of a sudden they would sidle up to me and say, "By the way, how do you join this church, anyway?" That was my signal that the testing truth had been passed. What is the testing truth for secular people? Whether or not there is a God and whether or not it matters. Adventists often think of the Sabbath, the state of the dead, and tithing as testing truths for people. But secular people are rarely worried about such things. The great testing truth for them is *whether there is a God and whether God matters in their lives.* When secular people become convinced that they have met God in your church, they are wide open. I usually responded to their request about joining the church with, "Got some time Tuesday night? I'll drop by and talk to you about it." I brought the baptismal vows, read them through, and offered to study any areas in which they were unclear or unprepared to make a commitment.

Every church needs to have a door through which secular people can enter and find their unique needs met. That door could be a special kind of worship service once a month or even once a quarter. It could be a second service at another time, like Sunday morning or Wednesday or Friday evening. It could take the form of small-group seminars or discussions. But every church that does not have the sole mission of outreach to the unchurched needs to provide ways in which secular people can be integrated and grown into Adventist ways of thinking and doing—a half-way house. Ultimately, of course, they should be encouraged to attend the Sabbath-morning worship service whether or not it feeds them, because the body needs to get together and worship on a regular basis. You need to be there because you are a part of the body. But the subculture may always remain the place where their primary spiritual needs are met.

Does allowing for a variety of spiritual experiences and expressions in a church lead to social and doctrinal chaos? It need not. Although there is only *one* gospel, it can and must be expressed in a variety of ways. Have you ever wondered why there are four Gospels in the New Testament when there was only one Jesus? I believe there is a very simple reason for it. The Lord Himself realized that there was no one presentation of the gospel that would meet all minds and all needs. It takes a variety of approaches to reach everyone. No single approach will ever be sufficient.

Madison Avenue is well aware of this. Did you know

that Colgate, Close-Up, and Ultra-Brite toothpastes are all made up with essentially the same ingredients? But they are not marketed the same way. Colgate emphasizes MFP—maximum fluoride protection. Who is interested in that? The "health nuts," people who are concerned about the health of their teeth. They delight in a toothpaste that will keep them out of the dentist's chair. Close-Up and Ultra-Brite have the same amount of fluoride, but the people who buy them are not interested in fluoride. Close-Up is marketed to people who like to get "close up," romantic types who are concerned about their breath. So Close-Up emphasizes the breath-freshening qualities of the toothpaste. Colgate has those too. But the people who buy Colgate are less interested in getting close up than they are in the health of their teeth. Ultra-Brite is for the vain types who are concerned about their appearance and like to have bright and shiny teeth. Madison Avenue has discovered that the people who buy Colgate would never dream of buying Close-Up. And the people who buy Ultra-Brite have no interest in the others. The three toothpastes are identical. But each one is *marketed* to a different class of people.

I think we should learn something from that. There is only one gospel. There is only one Jesus Christ. But there are many types of people, and Christ relates to each type in their own place and in their own time. Our greatest need may be to learn how to take this one gospel that we all believe in and present it to unique people in a way that meets their felt needs. Adventists with a passion for secular and unchurched people need to get together with others who share their passion and begin to brainstorm a little bit. What can we do differently in our church? What are the groups in our community that we are not reaching? Are we truly open as a church to new directions, or would a subculture be the way to start?

This book has been intended, not as a specific agenda for every situation, but as a large overview of the existing situation, with suggestions in broad strokes regarding things that can make a difference in a local church. The specifics of implementation will need to be worked out on a church-by-church basis.

14

And Now, Some Good News

I must close with some good news about the role of the church in a secular world. A number of trends suggest that better days for outreach to secular people are arriving. There is a growing backlash against secularism in the world today. People seem less concerned with appearances and the trappings of success than with self-fulfillment. Many are giving up raises and promotions for a simpler life with more time for human relationships.

There was a time when sociologists felt that secularization was an unstoppable process that would continue until all religion in the world was forever banished from human consciousness. That is now understood to have been naïve. Secularization seems to be a self-limiting phenomenon. Whenever it reaches a certain point, an inevitable backlash against it sets in. It is clear, not only in the former Soviet Bloc, but also in first-world areas like Western Europe and North America, that secular people have an increasing interest in the supernatural and in the development of the spiritual side of human life.

The search for a supernatural experience has taken some bizarre turns with the New Age and the influx of Eastern religions, but faith is an increasingly acceptable stance with secular people. Although the secular search for faith continues to exhibit barriers toward established

Christianity, faith-talk in a proper social context is more welcome than it used to be. (See *Newsweek*, 17 December 1990, 50-56, for a most interesting article on baby boomers and the church.) The explosive growth of strange cults illustrates the incredible power associated with meeting people's felt needs. How much better it would be if meeting felt needs led to an appreciation of the true gospel!

According to surveys, half of the unchurched in America would be open to the "right kind" of invitation to attend church, and 75 percent would be willing to send their children. It seems that few people are unchurched by choice. The biggest reason why people drop out is that they moved and never got around to finding a church in their new neighborhood.

Even more interesting is the fact that the majority of Americans brought up in irreligious homes are now members of some church. And half of unchurched people admit that they think about their need to go to church at least once a week. These facts indicate that the unchurched are not nearly as hardened as is generally assumed, but can be reached in caring ways that are sensitive to the hurts and the irritations that they have experienced in their relation with churches and churched people. Even small steps in the direction of making churches more user-friendly to secular people may be amply rewarded. It appears that a high-tech society, where artificial voices tell you to press whole series of buttons before you can contact a human being, has created an intense hunger for social and spiritual relationships.

Another sign that things are moving in a positive direction is that, while many mainline denominations decline, evangelical churches that are not excessively hidebound by traditional ways of doing things are growing rapidly in all sectors of society (see *User-Friendly Churches*, by George Barna, which is listed in the bibliography). A stunning example of this is the Willow Creek Community Church near Chicago. The church was started by a young pastor named Bill Hybels, who was driven by an experience he had had as a teenager in high school. His best friend was a totally secular person. One day the secular friend's girlfriend left him, and he was devastated. In agony he came to Bill and said, "Bill, I want to go to church with you." He was suddenly open to church because of this tragedy in his life.

So Bill took him to church, a Dutch Reformed Church. Dutch Reformed churches were molded from the very same kind of culture that most Adventist churches were—straight-laced, quiet as a mouse, traditional, everything taking place formally and in order. That is not wrong in itself, but it does not usually appeal to secular people. The two were not in church for five minutes before Hybels sensed that he had made a big mistake. For the first time he saw the church service through the eyes of someone who was hurting and searching for God. And there was nothing there for his friend. For three weeks after that the friend avoided him. Finally young Hybels cornered him and asked, "Look, what's going on? Why are you avoiding me?"

The friend said, "You know, I've always been friends with you, and I always thought you were a pretty cool guy. But I have to be honest with you. What you guys do in church is just not normal." He had been so stunned by the church experience, he no longer knew whether Bill was normal enough to be his friend. And Hybels vowed that one day he would start a church where people like his friend could feel comfortable, where they would not be so turned off by the peripherals that they could not find Christ.

A few years later he and a group of youth went to the most affluent suburb of Chicago and started knocking on doors, saying, "Do you go to church?"

"Yes, I do."

"Thank you very much. Keep it up. Goodbye."

Next door, "Do you go to church?"

"No, I don't."

"Why not?" They noted all the reasons people gave for staying away from church. Then they asked, "What kind of church would make you willing to try again?"

Together they designed a church that avoids the little irritations that unnecessarily turn off secular people. With little signals such as architecture, drama, and choice of music, they tell seekers that they understand the struggles of contemporary life, and that the gospel to be preached can make all the difference in the 1990s. Contrary to what most Adventists would expect, Willow Creek offers no soft religion. In order to be accepted as a member, you must attend faithfully for a year, become involved in a small group, and have a clearly identifiable ministry! This is no easy way to join a church! You have to be making a difference for Christ in your world before you can become a member of that church. And the standard is high; the elders of the church spend more time dealing with adultery than any other issue. Yet the average weekend attendance is more than fifteen thousand. And the offerings total more than $200,000 a week. They baptize a thousand people a year, 65 percent of them from unchurched, secular backgrounds.

The best-known part of the "Willow Creek strategy" is what they call a "Seeker Service." In addition to their regular worship service for believers, they offer a service specially designed for secular people. It is attractive and contemporary, so that secular people do not feel that they must enter a time warp in order to become a Christian. The little offensive things that needlessly turn people away are eliminated, opening the way for them to be challenged by the centrality of the gospel rather than by peripherals that they would perceive as meaningless without a prior acceptance of the gospel.

But the secret of Willow Creek's success is not so much the strategy as the sense of God's presence that one experiences there. You find yourself in the midst of a people for whom God is living and powerful. Adventists know how to talk *about* God, and *about* the Bible. But secular people who decide to join a church, don't want another secular, intellectual philosophy. They join because they have experienced the presence of a living God there.

It is not my purpose to extol Willow Creek as *the* model for Christianity or for Adventism at the turn of the millennium. The pastors of Willow Creek themselves warn that such single-mindedness would be a mistake. For one thing, we live in a diverse world where few strategies target more than a very narrow audience. For all its success with secular people, Willow Creek is making as little inroad into the African-American community as the Adventist Church is currently making in the Caucasian-American community. A person attending services at Willow Creek will also learn relatively little about doctrine or Bible prophecy. This means that Adventists cannot limit themselves to Willow Creek's approach. Nevertheless, Willow Creek's success demonstrates that the basic thesis of this book will work. A church that combines practical spirituality with a sensitivity to the secular mind can reach secular people in large numbers. Secular ministry *does* work.

For all of its shortcomings, the goal of this book is the fulfilling of Jesus' Great Commission in Matthew 28:18-20. In that passage Jesus commands His followers to go into all the world and seek disciples from every people group, including those of a secular mind-set. But it is not to be a human effort alone. It is the authority of Jesus (verse 18) that provides the power to make disciples. And Jesus promises that His presence (verse 20) will be with His followers as they go out to make disciples. To attempt, therefore, to carry out the strategy of this book without the spiritual component would be to fail entirely. On the other hand, 1 Corinthians 9 makes clear that to make no attempt to understand and approach these people groups in all of their God-given variety is to minimize the results that would otherwise be possible. Although the challenges of secular ministry are great, the basic mandate is clear. A genuine walk with God, combined with a strategy that is sensitive to the world in which we live, has the potential to make a mighty impact on this planet.

We are living at the turn of the ages. This is not so because an arbitrary number (A.D. 2000) is coming up. Rather, it is so because society is going through changes more wrenching than any that have been seen for hundreds of years. We are moving from the Industrial Age into the Information Age. History tells us that in times of wrenching change, people feel lost and nothing works right. Events and the growth of knowledge accelerate with frightening speed. Time seems to rush by out of control. People are adrift in a maelstrom of change. But history also tells us that societies like this can be uniquely open to a word from the Lord.

Although it would be more comfortable to retreat as we anticipate the battles ahead, the One who is on our side is bigger than the challenges that face us. Let us, therefore, be bold and seize the day!

Appendixes

Appendix A

The Spiritual Decision Process Chart

Since James F. Engel's book *Contemporary Christian Communications* has been out of print for some time, this appendix summarizes information related to Engel's major contribution, the Spiritual Decision Process Chart, which is reproduced on the following page. The chart enables the Christian witness to determine a person's spiritual location on a scale that runs from a total lack of the knowledge of God to fully devoted service to Christ. The goal of the Christian working with secular people is to help them move down the chart to a decision for Christ.

The stimulus to make spiritual progress originates with *need* activation (becoming aware of a felt need), for people do not change unless that change is seen to benefit them in some tangible way. The activation of a need leads to a *search for information*, which can result in a change of *beliefs*, which normally leads to a change of *attitudes*, which leads to a change in *behavior*. At this point a person is close to a decision which, when taken, leads to *spiritual growth*.

Decisions for Christ usually involve a lifetime process with many influences. Such decisions do not normally take place without some prior understanding of the gospel and its relevance for the individual's own life. Thus patience is

The Complete Spiritual Decision Process Model Showing the Stages of Spiritual Growth			
God's Role	**Communicator's Role**		**Human Response**
General Revelation		-8	**Awareness of Supreme Being**
Conviction	Proclamation	-7	Some knowledge of the gospel
		-6	Knowledge of the fundamentals of the gospel
		-5	Grasp of the personal implications of the gospel
		-4	Positive attitude toward the act of becoming a Christian
	Call for decision	-3	Problem recognition and intention to act
		-2	Decision to act
		-1	Repentance and faith in Christ
Regeneration			**New Creature**
Sanctification	Follow-up	+1	Post-decision evaluation
		+2	Incorporation into the church
	Cultivation	+3	Conceptual and behavioral growth • Communion with God • Stewardship • Internal reproduction • External reproduction
		•	
		•	
		Eternity	

necessary in working with secular people who do not have such a prior understanding.

People are open to an evangelistic approach when they have enough knowledge of the gospel to perceive that it is relevant to their basic needs. Since surveys indicate that the majority of Americans have only a moderate amount of knowledge of the gospel (-7), knowledge building is where most Christian communication must begin. The role of the Christian witness for people at levels -7 and -6, therefore, is to build awareness of the basic tenets of the gospel. At these levels a call for decision is inappropriate.

The upper part of the chart has at least two other implications for evangelism. For one thing, since there is little in the way of literature or packaged approaches for people in levels -8 to -6, most Christians are totally unprepared to cope with the majority of people they meet. Second, evangelistic "success" must not be evaluated only in terms of decisions. Many will never see large numbers of decisions because they are dealing with people who are at the upper levels of the chart. Evangelism should be considered successful if people move down the chart, whether or not a decision has yet been made.

People with a positive attitude toward the gospel (-4) are the people who are nearing approachability for decision.

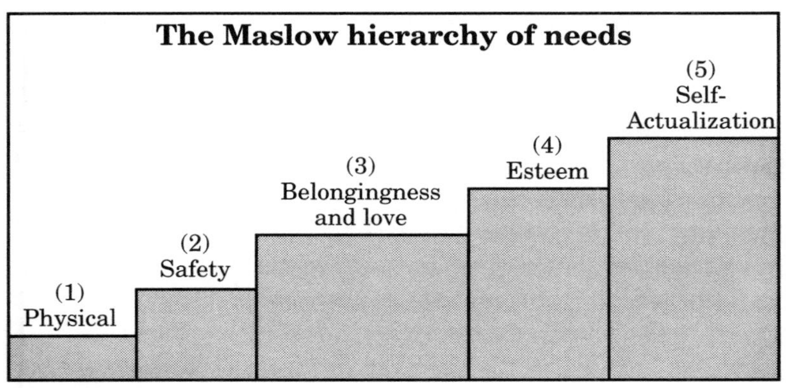

They are ready for the call at the level of problem recognition (-3), which means perceiving a difference between one's own life and the ideal life defined by Scripture.

Need activation

People generally will not change unless they feel the need to change. Thus, the first step in helping people to progress in the spiritual decision-making process is the activation of need. Anyone can be reached, provided he or she is reached at the level of felt needs.

Operating on the basis of Maslow's hierarchy, Engel articulates three basic needs: survival needs (1 and 2); needs related to acceptance by the involvement with others (3 and 4); and needs centering around individual competency and self-expression (5).

In much of the world, life is dominated by physical hardships. In such situations people are profoundly unhappy; life is a bleak and frustrating experience. The first obligation of the church in such areas is to remedy the underlying conditions (see Luke 4:18, 19), and where that is impossible, to emphasize the rewards of the next life.

The awareness of need is often precipitated by a catastrophic event in a person's life. Such an event can lead to a crumbling of the defense mechanisms that mask a person's awareness of need. The chart on pages 223 and 224 can help the church to assess the level of catastrophic stress that people are experiencing. A score of several hundred points within a given year is not unusual, and this would point to an almost devastating level of stress.

Various stages in the life cycle are also times when people are open to change. In the chart on page 225, Engel offers a generalized overview of the typical North American life cycle. Stages 2 and 5 tend to be the most resistant to change, while stages 1 and 4 are the most open to change. Special needs in stage 4 are strengthening marriage, teaching values to children, and finding satisfaction on the job.

Information search

When people discover unmet needs in their lives, they begin what Engel calls the search process. They actively seek information that will help them meet those needs. The search process will cover as many sources as are available to the individual, including electronic media, books, magazines, advice of friends, and, if the need is pressing, even strangers. The greatest opportunity to reach secular people comes in providing needed information at the right time. An appropriate use of magazine ads, radio spots, and creative self-help books, therefore, can arouse interest in people whose search for information has been activated by a felt need.

Tract distribution, on the other hand, is largely a waste of time and money, according to Engel, unless the tracts are specifically aimed at a felt need of the person receiving the tract. Even then, a tract is most likely to be read when it was received from a trusted personal friend rather than from a stranger on the street or in a passing car. Christian television must also be combined with face-to-face witness in order to be evangelistically effective.

Formation and change of beliefs and attitudes

At the point of information search it becomes possible for a person's attitudes and beliefs to progress in the spiritual decision process toward a decision for Christ.

Belief, according to Engel, is something a person holds to be true with respect to a given subject or action. Attitude is a positive or negative evaluation about a given action that is usually consistent with a person's beliefs. Intention relates to the subjective probability that beliefs and attitudes will be acted on.

The probability that a person will change his or her beliefs is directly proportional to the credibility of the sender. This credibility is determined less by words than by the character of the sender's life. Generally speaking, people change in very small amounts at a given time.

Decision

While psychology is helpful at many points in the decision-making process, conversion is a divine work. The Christian's part in the secular person's decision-making process is gentle, friendly encouragement. Persuasion is up to God alone (see 2 Tim. 2:24-26). While not all Christians are evangelists, all are to be witnesses (see 1 Pet. 3:15).

Spiritual growth

Growth toward Christian spiritual maturity is stimulated by failure. So a teaching and training program to develop Christian maturity should also begin at the point of felt needs. Rapidly growing churches are characterized by a need-centered ministry. Surveys and visitation can be used to find out what doctrinal, felt needs, and behavioral issues are affecting a congregation at a particular time. Preaching, to be effective today, must be based on accurate feedback.

Conclusion

This brief summary of Engel's book only suggests the valuable insights available in it if a reader can find a copy in a good library or used bookstore. The basic points summarized here supplement the material in chapters 9 and 10. Further information on the practical "how-tos" of secular ministry is available in the annotated bibliography.

The effect of change on social readjustment

Life Event	Mean Value
1. Death of a spouse	100
2. Divorce	73
3. Marital separation from mate	65
4. Detention in jail or other institution	63
5. Death of a close family member	63
6. Major personal injury or illness	53
7. Marriage	50
8. Being fired at work	47
9. Marital reconciliation with mate	45
10. Retirement from work	45
11. Major change in the health or behavior of family member	44
12. Pregnancy	40
13. Sexual difficulties	39
14. Gaining a new family member (e.g., through birth, adoption, oldster moving in, marriage, etc.)	39
15. Major business readjustment (e.g., merger, reorganization, bankruptcy, etc.)	39
16. Major change in financial state (e.g., a lot worse off or a lot better off than usual)	38
17. Death of a close friend	37
18. Changing to a different line of work	36
19. Major change in the number of arguments with spouse (e.g., either a lot more or a lot less than usual regarding child rearing, personal habits, etc.)	35
20. Taking on a mortgage greater than $10,000 (e.g., purchasing a home, business, etc.)	31
21. Foreclosure on a mortgage or loan	30
22. Major change in responsibilities at work (e.g., promotion, demotion, lateral transfer)	29
23. Son or daughter leaving home (e.g., marriage, college)	29
24. In-law troubles	29
25. Outstanding personal achievement	28
26. Wife beginning or ceasing work outside the home	26

27. Beginning or ceasing formal schooling 26
28. Major change in living conditions (e.g., building new home, remodeling, deterioration of home or neighborhood) 25
29. Revision of personal habits (dress, manners, etc.) 24
30. Trouble with the boss 23
31. Major change in working hours or conditions 20
32. Change in residence 20
33. Changing to a new school 20
34. Major change in usual type and/or amount of recreation 19
35. Major change in church activities (e.g., lot more or less than usual) 19
36. Major change in social activities (e.g., clubs, movies, dances) 18
37. Taking on a mortgage or loan less than $10,000 (car, TV) 17
38. Major change in sleeping habits (e.g., a lot more or less than usual, or change in part of day when asleep) 16
39. Major change in number of family get-togethers (more or less) 15
40. Major change in eating habits (more or less, or different) 15
41. Vacation 13
42. Christmas 12
43. Minor violations of the law (e.g., traffic tickets, jaywalking, disturbing the peace, etc.) 11

Stages in the "passage" through the life cycle

1. **Pulling Up Roots.** 18-22. A transition from parents' beliefs to the establishment of new, strictly personal beliefs. Often characterized by an identity crisis.

2. **Building the Dream.** 22-30. "Forming the dream" and working one's aspirations through occupational and marital choices. Much importance placed on "doing what we should."

3. **Living Out the Dream.** 30-35. Putting down roots, living out one's aspirations, and making them become a reality.

4. **Midlife Transition.** 35-45. Reassessment of the dream and the values that have been internalized. A final casting aside of inappropriate role models. Equilibrium will be restored either through a renewal or a resignation to the realities of life.

5. **Middle Adulthood.** 45-59. Reduced personal striving and more emphasis on living consistently with a clarified code of values, placing more importance on personal relationships and individual fulfillment.

6. **Late Adult Transition.** 60-65 and beyond. Diminished active occupational life and eventual retirement. Retirement can either lead to renewal or resignation.

Beliefs, attitudes, intentions, and the spiritual decision process

-8	Awareness of a supreme Being	Knowledge
-7	Some knowledge of the gospel	Knowledge
-6	Knowledge of the fundamentals of the gospel	Knowledge
-5	Grasp of the personal implications of the gospel	Belief
-4	Positive attitude toward the act of becoming a Christian	Attitude
-3	Problem recognition and intention to act	Intention
-2	Decision to act	Decision
-1	Repentance and faith in Christ	
	New creature	

Appendix B

Adventist Administration in a Secular World

It is with considerable trepidation that I add this appendix to the book. I have had little experience in administration, and I do not consider myself particularly gifted in that field. It would be much simpler to avoid this aspect of the topic. But I have come to realize over the years that administrative policies and practices make a big difference in whether or not God's people can effect constructive change. Not only is this true, but experience teaches me that an administrative structure that is not continually renewing itself on the basis of changing realities in the world is ultimately doomed to failure. It is my hope that what follows will stimulate constructive discussions.

Some of the following suggestions are offered in the hope of streamlining our approach to secular people. Others seem to be called for by the circumstances of the world's plunge into the Information Age. To those with administrative responsibilities I can only say, Take what seems worth using, and ignore the rest.

The Information Age

Society is now passing through a social revolution equal in magnitude to the Industrial Revolution 200 years ago. Prior to the eighteenth century most people were employed in agriculture. But thanks to the advances of the Industrial Age, fewer than 3 percent of today's Americans produce far more food than we can eat.

Just as the age of agriculture passed away some time ago, the industrial age now seems to be fading out as well.[1] Less than 10 percent of Americans are needed to manufacture all the goods sold in the United States.[2] Virtually all newly created jobs are in the area of services, particularly the creation, processing, and distribution of information.[3] The new wealth of society is not money or raw materials. It is information.[4]

In the pre-Industrial Age, power resided in the ownership and processing of raw materials. Work was labor-intensive, meaning that goods received value from the time and energy invested by human beings in creating the product (handmade). Political dominance usually went to the most fertile and well-watered areas of the world, such as the Fertile Crescent in the ancient Middle East—Egypt and Babylon in particular.

In the Industrial Age, power resided in the ownership and utilization of energy sources, by which human time and energy could be multiplied in the mass production of goods. Work was capital-intensive, meaning that goods received value to the extent that people invested money in the procuring and efficient utilization of energy sources. Political dominance went to nations that achieved high levels of manufacturing efficiency (like Germany, the U.S., and Japan) and that developed large banking centers (like New York and London).

In the Information Age, on the other hand, power resides in the ownership of information and the ability to process and distribute that information. Work is knowledge-intensive, meaning that goods receive value to the extent that they are invested with the best and the latest ideas. Political dominance will go to those nations that provide a climate of free thought and easy interaction between thinkers, for it is in the interaction of thinkers that ideas are honed and created.[5]

What impact should these and other societal trends have on those responsible for the shape of Adventist administration in the nineties and beyond? What kinds of changes might help the church to accomplish its mission more effectively?

Administrative style

The Industrial Age called for an authoritarian style of administration. The ideal workers in a mass-production environment were those who didn't think for themselves, but were like interchangeable parts, offering a minimum of conflict and disagreement, working on rigid time schedules in massive, centralized institutions.

But the old mass-production strategies do not seem to be working well anymore. The information society thrives when control is decentralized. The most valuable employee is no longer the "yes man" of the Industrial Age, but is a person willing to question and challenge. Employee initiative, creativity, diversity, knowledge, and education are at a premium, and the ability to work with people is often far more valuable than skill at manipulating things.[6]

The best ideas seem to be moving up from the bottom rather than down from the top.[7] The most successful corporations are those that not only tolerate, but learn to encourage creative and "difficult" people. This is so not only because people want to be part of the decision-making process, but because creative and difficult people stimulate the creation of ideas when given an environment where open and free discussion is encouraged.

We are seeing, therefore, a trend from representative democracy to participatory democracy.[8] When people whose lives are affected by decisions become a part of the process of arriving at those decisions, they support them with enthusiasm. In the political realm this can be seen in the proliferation of popular initiatives and the increasing trend toward government by referendum.

The above realities may be perceived as threatening in the setting of a church office, particularly where adherence to a creed or tradition is the paramount consideration in hiring and firing. I certainly do not want to suggest that we relax doctrinal and lifestyle standards (as I believe I have argued strongly in the main text of this book). However, we may want to consider ways that faithful but "difficult" pastors and lay people can be made to feel more at home in our midst. The people who are often shunted to one side in the name of harmony might be the very ones who could save us from staleness in life, teaching, and administrative procedure.

From my own experience, I can say that I learn much more from those I disagree with than from those I agree with. Some of my most fruitful relationships have been with people who initially seemed troublesome and obtuse. As underlined in the main text of this book, the secular, information society in which we live requires a dedication to listening and learning if we are to operate at peak efficiency. We must not only draw close to those we wish to serve, but also to those with whom we are serving.

Networking

The increasing failure of the authoritarian structures of the Industrial Age to govern society effectively has caused people to set up networks—informal mechanisms for finding and passing on information, ideas, and resources. As a result of the proliferation of knowledge and information at the present time, "loners" have a hard time getting the kind of input that is necessary for making sound decisions. Today's administrator needs input and constructive criticism from a wide variety of sources if he or she is to make wise and fair decisions. More and more administrators, therefore, are reaching outside the usual channels for the information and help they need. The most helpful exchanges of all may take place with individuals whose expertise lies far outside our own area of interest.

The committee system of the Adventist Church has the inherent potential to foster the interdisciplinary interchange so critical to sound decision-making in the Information Age, but the fact that the system often does not work indicates a need for reform. Ways must be found to provide our leading thinkers with the opportunity to interact more with each other and with significant critics from among the laity in the church. The current "youth cabinet" approach of the General Conference president is an example of how structured networking can enhance the functioning of administration.

One reason the networking system of committees does not always work well may be that the structures of Adventist administration have become too rigid. The purpose of administrative structure is to foster efficiency of operation. When these structures become barriers to efficiency, they no longer serve their intended purpose. As conduits of finance and political clout, administrative structures can get in the way of people who need to interact with each other in order to fulfill the great commission.

Let me illustrate. In large cities Adventists from as many as twelve churches that are associated with three or four conferences may live in a particular neighborhood. They drive in all directions to go to church because they like a particular preacher or a certain style of worship or Sabbath school, or because friends and/or relatives attend there. Church attendance in a big city is rarely related to a burden for a particular neighborhood. Thus, church evangelistic programs that center on the neighborhood of the church (where few members may live) do not always attract the members' interest. The members' evangelistic burden is the place where they live and their personal network of acquaintances (including workmates), friends, and family.

If we can find ways to bridge some of these artificial church and conference barriers, we could organize people from different churches and conferences to work together and develop a burden for a particular neighborhood. Evangelism in the Information Age will be increasingly neighborhood- and workplace-oriented, with less focus on a church building as the unifying location for outreach, unless the very worship service itself becomes a drawing card to the wider community.

Relational focus

Although the mass-production workplace may not have been geared toward it, one of the fundamental assumptions of industrial society was individualism.[9] This resulted in the obsession with self-fulfillment that was characteristic of the seventies,[10] not to mention the self-absorption of the baby-boomers who came of age in the eighties. But there is a rapidly increasing emphasis on the development of personal relationships and group interaction.[11] This emphasis seems related to the onset of the Information Age.

It was thought at one time that the Information Age would produce a cold and impersonal society, *1984* style, of machinelike "technocrats." The opposite seems to be occurring. Wherever the new impersonal information technologies are introduced, the result seems to be humanization of that technology. For example, the rise of the super–high tech modern hospital with its cold, impersonal efficiency has been accompanied by trends such as the proliferation of hospices and birthing centers, and the return of the family doctor.[12] People are not satisfied with material success and workplace efficiency. There is an increasing hunger for personal relationships and group interaction.

The societal trend toward interpersonal, small-group structures and self-help efforts is encouraging, since the Adventist Church is stocked with a wealth of good approaches. Health programs, Bible seminars, and Sabbath School discussion groups can be a great way to meet the need for fellowship while helping people learn how to think along new lines. But the corresponding trend in society to move away from institutional help in the direction of self-help indicates that such programs will succeed only to the extent that they utilize and energize the lay people of a church. Clergy are often distrusted in today's society, on the assumption that they have a vested interest in fostering the growth of a church or religious system. The most powerful argument for Christianity in our world is the impact that the faith has on nonprofessional church people. Thus, motivating and training the laity for secular witnessing is crucial.

Global economy

The information revolution is resulting in a trend toward a world economy or globalization.[13] A car can now be put together from parts manufactured on nearly every continent. Thanks to satellite technology, information is now universally and instantly available, making it possible for all nations to have an equal crack at the "capital" of this new trend in history.[14] No one part of the earth is inherently at an advantage in the procuring and processing of ideas.

The trend toward a world economy underlines the need to increase the transfer of leadership and ideas in more than one direction (the usual mode of transfer in Adventism is from "first world" to "third world"). There is, probably, no other church that has as great an opportunity to be the first truly "world church" as the Seventh-day Adventist Church. However, our ninety-year-old administrative structure seems increasingly out of step with the corresponding trends toward decentralization and participatory democracy. We need more encouragement of local initiative, more interchange of ideas from bottom to top, and less hierarchical direction.

As globalization increases, there is a countertrend toward cultural assertiveness. People want to touch base with their roots. As a church we have the biblical mandate to affirm, on the one hand, the unity of all peoples in Christ, while at the same time affirming that the gospel is best offered to the world by a diverse, cosmopolitan people with representatives who feel at home in any culture.

Future orientation

Long-term strategies tend to increase short-term costs, and therefore are usually avoided by government and business, and also churches. The speed with which change comes in the Information Age, however, forces institutions into a future orientation.[15] Success is possible only through the anticipation of trends—the ability to anticipate where the "market" will be in ten years and to position oneself to take advantage of it by appropriate long-range planning.[16] Information has become more crucial to success than money (witness such firms as Intel, Xerox, and Apple Computer). George Barna's book *Frog in the Kettle* (listed in the bibliography) is an excellent example of recent attempts to anticipate where the church needs to be ten years from now.

It might be well, therefore, for the Seventh-day Adventist Church to set up an ongoing, future-oriented "think tank" to help it respond ahead of time to societal trends instead of being dragged from one crisis to another. Such a department should employ at least one full-time individual who is trained in both theology and sociology, and whose responsibility is to research trends and advise the church on appropriate planning.

A major issue regarding the future of the church is the shape that it will take ten or twenty years from now, should the Lord delay His coming. (I don't hope for such a delay, but experience teaches that it is far from impossible.) There are several options. The church can take the "lean, mean" approach of doctrinal and lifestyle purity, restricting its membership to a small group of fully committed people. Such a church will fail to have a broad impact on the various segments of society. Another option is to see in the diversity of secular society the need for a corresponding openness and diversity in the church. This will make it possible for the church to have a major impact on contemporary society. The third option, which is the easiest and most natural, is to simply drift into the future. This option is far more dangerous than either of the others.

One of the goals of this book is to challenge the church to make conscious decisions about the shape that it will take in the future. The strategy outlined in the main body of this book is an attempt to take the best of both the "lean/mean" and the "openness/diversity" options. Whether this is truly possible in the real world we will know only if we try, but if we fail to try, we will consign ourselves to the secular drift that has already taken a devastating toll on our mission.

Education

Another trend in North American society is an increasing reaction to information overload. There is a desire to sift and order information, even if one must go outside of one's own discipline to find the key.[17] In such a setting the university plays a central role as the place where knowledge is codified, tested, and made available to all comers. Thus the Adventist Church's strong emphasis on higher education has the potential to keep our church at the cutting edge of societal change. In fact, in many developing countries Seventh-day Adventists are taking the educational lead. In such countries Adventist education may be approaching its finest hour. In North America, however, there is a great need for increasing interaction between educators and administrators so that maximum advantage can be taken of our achievements in higher education.

Efficiency

Since the economic boom times seem to be gone for a while (and perhaps permanently), we need greater administrative efficiency. Information Age methods and technology may provide just such efficiency. Computer networking, fax machines, and other cutting-edge information technologies will enable the church to streamline offices and put more personnel back into the field where the real action of church growth is taking place. In the Industrial Age it made sense to put your best people in offices. This ensured the smooth functioning of the administrative machine. In the Information Age, the best people will increasingly be needed in pulpits and other ministries at the grass-roots level.

It is quite possible that new organizational structures will emerge that emphasize local initiative and networking. For example, metropolitan New York City covers more than twenty counties in three states, and is serviced by five conferences and two unions. It would seem wise, therefore, to consider the possibility of reorienting the administrative structure so that it is more mission driven. This would make it possible to focus on the changing realities in the neighborhood and the workplace rather than on political or ethnic boundaries. A single office might accomplish the work of seven, with no loss of efficiency in fulfilling the basic mission of the church.

Spiritual tone

The fact that the church is no longer at the center of society's focus in a secular age may be a hidden blessing.[18] The Christian church in general has lost most of its former societal responsibilities: education, care of the sick and the elderly, social control, and political influence. Thus, it has been thrown back to its religious task, and it must, therefore, justify its existence in spiritual terms alone.[19] The church must depend more and more on its inward resources of faith.

In an anti-institutional age, the church must move more to the servant role and away from the authority role. Secular people have not rejected the true faith as much as the institutional trappings that tend to come with it.[20] To reach such people, ministers and people must be fellow pilgrims. The authoritarian approach is no longer acceptable.[21]

The upshot of all this is that we seem to have come full circle, back to the situation of the church in the society of the first century. If so, then the answer to secularization is a return to the spirit of the early church as it appears in Acts 2 through 4. This could be summarized as (1) "devotion to the apostle's teaching," (2) "fellowship," (3) prayer, (4) the sacraments, and (5) economic commitment.[22] The return to small groups, Bible seminars, and help for people who are struggling physically and spiritually are all part of the package.

Personnel management

A real tragedy in Adventism is that when secular ministries are developed, they often prove to be temporary because the pastor who follows in the same church is not as sensitive to the unique dynamic that has developed in that church. The new pastor may be unable to appreciate the exciting diversity that the Spirit brings. He or she may confront creative people as "heretics" who need to be moved out of office or even out of the church. I have heard new Adventist Christians, who were once excited to be part of a growing and dynamic community, say with tears in their eyes, "We still love the Lord and we still love the church, but we don't know how much longer we can stand this." One reason the explosive growth of churches like Willow Creek rarely happens in the Adventist Church is that the frequent changeovers in pastoral personnel at the local church level produce a lack of the continuity of vision that secular ministry requires.

Several administrative strategies may have to be implemented before secular ministry in the Adventist Church can produce the results that have occurred in other settings such as Willow Creek. One of these is to allow longer terms of service in a given church for pastors who want to develop a ministry to the secular community. It takes time for the pastor's vision to permeate the church. Willow Creek's pastors suggest that it generally takes six years, which means that the most fruitful results would take place from the seventh year on. Providing longer terms of service in one church for pastors with a vision for ministry to the secular community should result in significant church growth.

A second strategy for supporting secular outreach would be a more careful mating of churches and pastors. Just as individual Christians have unique gifts and personalities, so churches seem to have unique personalities and possibilities for outreach. In most cases, joining pastors and churches with vastly differing visions and expectations is a prescription for failure.

A third strategy is to help local churches develop a clear and ongoing sense of their unique mission that can transcend the ebb and flow of pastoral visions and programs. A church that knows where it is going can give more precise input in the pastoral selection process, and can help facilitate smoother changeovers when such are necessary.

Developing a secular ministry requires patience and time from the local church, from its pastor, and from the conference office that oversees both. Adventist pastors, however, are usually quite transient at the present time. Where the conference machinery is not set up with the above three strategies in mind, it is critical for pastors to function with their transience clearly in mind. If a pastor knows that he or she is likely to move on before a vision or a program can mature, he or she must take that into account in every decision. Such pastors will need to ensure the durability of every program or strategy that is developed in the local church. If a program or outreach cannot outlast a change in leadership, it might best be left unstarted.

Churches need to become increasingly self-sufficient in spiritual growth and in outreach. This is where elders and other church leaders become crucial. So-called lay people can make a lifetime mission out of their involvement in a local church. They provide the stability that secular outreach requires. Unfortunately, too many pastors perceive strong local leadership as an impediment to be overcome rather than an asset to be utilized, and this discourages local leaders and destroys continuity.

Perhaps the time has come to develop a network of Adventist pastors who have learned how to blend ministry to the secular culture with a sensitivity to the needs of the more traditional Adventist members in the church. Such pastors can enable a traditional church to be comfortable in accepting converts from the secular environment, and can enable such converts to be comfortable joining a fairly traditional church. Such "two-horizon" pastors, I believe, have a special talent. Not every pastor can reach across cultural barriers successfully. It would be helpful to conference presidents to have a talent bank to draw from when a church with a creative and successful outreach to the secular community needs a pastor who can help them continue that ministry.

Turn-of-the-century administrators

What kind of person do the above realities suggest is needed in Adventist administration? As we approach the end of this century, the most crucial qualification is "critical thinking." Critical thinking is the ability to analyze a wide range of options, including one's own preferences, with dispassionate objectivity. Critical thinkers seek to avoid gullibility, self-protection games, and political influence peddling. Critical thinkers don't think things are so because they have always thought so, nor do they do something "this way" because they have always done it that way. Critical thinkers fear stagnation more than they fear change. Such administrators will be fresh and creative in fostering outreach, and within the legitimate bounds set by inspiration, they will be ideologically flexible in their dealings with pastors and members who differ with them.

The ideal Adventist administrator will be increasingly open to counsel, especially from lay people with expertise in specific areas of conference need and concern. He or she will learn to tolerate "difficult" people who have the strength to speak their minds to a superior and confront problems head on. In this day and age, Adventist administrators cannot afford to be victims of the Saddam Hussein syndrome, where everybody knows the truth about a situation except the boss, but everyone is afraid to say it.

Successful administrators will seek the best information available for making decisions, whether it comes from books, journals, educational centers, superiors, inferiors, Adventists, or non-Adventists. They will not be afraid to study psychology and sociology, or to take surveys when necessary. They will learn to communicate in everyday language, rather than in Adventese or administratese.

Perhaps most important in fostering all of the above is a democratic administrative style that seeks consensus rather than acceptance, that emphasizes servant leadership rather than authoritarian pronouncements, and that seeks humility and authenticity rather than image-building. In the process we will discover that the best approach to these new realities is a renewed humility as we learn the lessons of inspiration, combined with a renewed love for the souls for whom Christ died.

Odds and ends

Another major trend today is toward multiple options rather than monolithic communities. In an age when people can choose from among scores of television channels, hundreds of compact music discs in dozens of musical styles, and tens of thousands of videos at the rental store, they are not likely to be satisfied with a church that has "only one song to sing." Here is where decentralizing at the local level can make a difference. The multiple gifts of the Spirit can enable a church to provide a varied menu of options for the diversity of people in its community.

Another current reality is that many individuals today find themselves "between the times," at home in neither the Industrial Age nor the Information Age, out of touch with both the youth and the elderly. Such individuals tend to live under a high level of stress, often to the point of disorientation.[23] Ongoing programs in time management, handling family stresses and dysfunctions, scheduling, financial management, and other practical, everyday subjects are no longer optional to a thriving local church ministry. "Practical godliness," as Ellen White liked to put it, must be at the cutting edge of ministry in the nineties. I have therefore made it a personal goal to produce a follow-up volume to this book in which the "how-tos" of practical godliness from an Adventist perspective can be laid out. The concept of "faith for today" has never been more relevant than right now.

In closing, I wish to emphasize that the above thoughts on administration are not as polished and thought through as the main body of this book. They may well need to be updated at points, since I developed many of these points more than five years ago. They are offered here, not as prescriptions, but as suggestions for consideration by those in administrative positions who want to make a difference in the Seventh-day Adventist Church.

---

1. Alvin Toffler, *The Third Wave* (New York: William Morrow, 1980), 26.
2. Ibid., 197.
3. John Naisbitt, *Megatrends* (New York: Warner Books, 1982), 14.
4. Ibid., 15.
5. The last three paragraphs are based in a general way on the analysis of Daniel Bell, *The Cultural Contradictions of Capitalism* (New York: Basic Books, 1976), 198. Because the book as a whole is somewhat dated and does not impact as largely on my overall thesis as others, it is not listed in the bibliography.
6. Toffler, 402, 403, 261-281; Bell, 146-148, 198.
7. Naisbitt, 97.
8. Ibid., 159.
9. Bell, 16.
10. Christopher Lasch, *The Culture of Narcissism* (New York: W. W. Norton, 1978), passim; see also Daniel Yankelovich, *New Rules: Searching for Self-fulfillment in a World Turned Upside Down* (New York: Random House, 1981), 4, 5.
11. Yankelovich, 251.
12. Naisbitt, 39. Note also the implications of recent movies like *Baby Boom* and *Curly Sue*.
13. Naisbitt, 76.
14. Ibid., 55.
15. Ibid., 18.
16. Ibid., 79.
17. Ibid., 189.
18. Lausanne Occasional Papers No. 8. *Christian Witness to Secularized People* (Wheaton, Ill.: Lausanne Committee for World Evangelization, 1980), 19.

19. Heije Faber, "The Ministry in a Changing Society," *Perkins Journal* 34 (Fall 1980), 9.
20. Gustav Wiencke, ed. *Christian Education in a Secular Society* (Philadelphia: Fortress Press, 1970), 114.
21. Faber, 20.
22. Lausanne No. 8, 20-22.
23. Toffler, 33.

Annotated Bibliography

Following is a list of books and journal articles that have been exceptionally helpful to me in wrestling with the issue of secularization and its impact on Adventist faith and practice. The list is definitely not complete (I have examined nearly a thousand items related to the subject), nor is it necessarily up to date on the latest editions. But many people have asked for a list of the sources that helped me to sharpen my ideas. The best sources that I am presently aware of are listed here.

Books

Barna, George. *The Frog in the Kettle*. Ventura, Calif.: Regal Books, 1990.

This books is somewhat like a Christian *Megatrends* (see below). Barna seeks to outline the kind of church that will make a difference in the society of the year 2000. The book will aid those who wish to be prepared ahead of time for the massive changes the Information Age continues to bring about.

________. *User-Friendly Churches*. Ventura, Calif.: Regal Books, 1991.

In the spirit of *A Search for Excellence,* Barna examines ten rapidly growing churches and compares them with a similar number of declining churches. He notes that all growing churches have certain things in common that declining churches do not and vice versa. A very provocative book for people interested in the local church.

Brinsmead, Robert D. *This Is Life*. Fallbrook, Calif.: Verdict Publications, 1978.

Although Brinsmead has, in the last decade, taken numerous positions in direct opposition to SDA beliefs, this little book from an earlier period of his life articulates a superb way of sharing the gospel with the nonreligious mind.

Campolo, Anthony. *A Reasonable Faith: Responding to Secularism*. Waco, Tex.: Word Books, 1983.

Immensely entertaining, as always, Campolo provides a superb, nontechnical analysis of the secular mentality. The book provides an excellent starting point for understanding the way a secular person thinks. Campolo's theological approaches to secular people are at times somewhat questionable from an Adventist perspective.

Coon, Glenn A. *Path to the Heart*. Washington, D.C.: Review and Herald, 1958.

The book is quaint and at times almost irritatingly childlike in its simplicity. Nevertheless, it pounds home as no other book does the Christlike way to approach individuals with the message of the gospel. My favorite "witnessing book." Particularly helpful for reaching out spiritually to family and friends.

Engel, James F. *Contemporary Christian Communications: Its Theory and Practice*. Nashville: Thomas Nelson, 1979.

See Appendix A.

Foster, Richard J. *Celebration of Discipline: The Path to Spiritual Growth*. San Francisco: Harper and Row, 1978.
Outstanding summary of the classic spiritual disciplines, such as meditation, prayer, fasting, solitude, and confession.

Gilder, George. *Microcosm: The Quantum Revolution in Economics and Technology*. New York: Simon and Schuster, 1989.
A fascinating look at the revolutionary impact of computerization, quantum mechanics, and the resulting Information Age on everything we hold dear today. As the student of Carver Mead, the "prophet" of the computer age, Gilder is well qualified to suggest where society is going from here. Although the book is not easy to read if one is not "into" computers, the concepts in this book will challenge every thoughtful Adventist, particularly church administrators.

Gilkey, Langdon Brown. *Naming the Whirlwind*. Indianapolis: Bobbs-Merrill, 1969.
This book contains the classic statement outlining the major characteristics of the secular world view. Although published nearly twenty years ago, this book is still a major starting point for any theological discussion of secularism.

Griffin, Emory A. *The Mind Changers: The Art of Christian Persuasion*. Wheaton, Ill.: Tyndale House, 1976.
A humorous and insightful survey of various methods of persuasion, including many pointed cartoons. Deals with some of the same concerns as Engel.

Hunter, James Davison. *American Evangelicalism: Conservative Religion and the Quandary of Modernity*. New Brunswick, N.J.: Rutgers University Press, 1983.

A research work of major importance to Adventists in America today. The author shows that, even though evangelicals fight against it, secularism affects everything that they do.

Hybels, Bill. *Too Busy Not to Pray: Slowing Down to Be With God*. Downer's Grove, Ill.: InterVarsity Press, 1988.

My favorite book on the devotional life. Contains very helpful guidelines for prayer and journaling. The author is the pastor of the Willow Creek Community Church. The illustration about the Buddhist neighbor in chapter 2 of this book is based largely on an illustration in one of Hybels's sermons.

________. *Honest to God? Becoming an Authentic Christian*. Grand Rapids, Mich.: Zondervan, 1990.

First-rate book on the issue of Christian genuineness and authenticity. The book challenges the reader to do whatever it takes to live Christian faith in direct contact with reality. Many conscious and unconscious ways that Christians use to live in denial of reality are exposed. Must reading for secular ministry!

Institute of Church Ministry. Andrews University. Berrien Springs, MI 49104-1500.

The place to write for information on demographic studies of the zip-code areas relevant to a local church. An excellent starting point for secular ministry.

Lausanne Occasional Papers No. 2. *The Willowbank Report: Gospel and Culture*. P.O. Box 1100, Wheaton, IL 60187: Lausanne Committee for World Evangelization, 1980.

Though brief, an excellent discussion of the interaction between the gospel and human cultures around the world.

Lausanne Occasional Papers No. 8. *Christian Witness to Secularized People*. P.O. Box 1100, Wheaton, IL 60187: Lausanne Committee for World Evangelization, 1980.

Perhaps the best summary, from an evangelical perspective, of the problems secularization creates for Christian faith and mission, this booklet also suggests some excellent methods for solving those problems. Short and to the point! The voted product of a group study.

Lewis, C. S. *Mere Christianity*. Macmillan Paperbacks Edition. New York: Macmillan, 1960.

Lewis is, perhaps, the most famous convert from atheism to Christianity in this century. His books wrestle powerfully with the kinds of issues that come up when Christians witness to secular people. *Mere Christianity* covers the essentials of basic Christianity in terms a secular person can appreciate.

Naisbitt, John. *Megatrends*. New York: Warner Books, 1982.

Although it has now been updated in a questionable way, the original *Megatrends* still provides a most insightful analysis (with a wealth of fascinating illustrations) of ten major trends that continue to shape American society today.

Princeton Religion Research Center. *The Unchurched American*. P.O. Box 389, Princeton, NJ 08542.

Presents the results of Gallup research concerning the unchurched and offers suggestions for reaching them.

Rasi, Humberto M., and Fritz Guy, eds. *Meeting the Secular Mind: Some Adventist Perspectives*. Berrien Springs, Mich.: Andrews University Press, 1985.

The starting point for any Seventh-day Adventist who is

interested in the problem of secularization or in methods designed to reach people of a secular mind-set.

Sahlin, Monte. *Friendship Evangelism Seminar*. Concerned Communications, 1989.

An excellent how-to seminar on how to present an effective verbal witness in secular situations, whether on the job or in everyday conversation. Provides the kind of detailed insight that could not be included in a book like this one.

Toffler, Alvin. *The Third Wave*. New York: William Morrow, 1980.

A sequel to Toffler's popular book *Future Shock*, *The Third Wave* describes the present development from the Industrial Age to the Information Age. As always, Toffler is interesting reading.

Yankelovich, Daniel. *New Rules: Searching for Self-fulfillment in a World Turned Upside Down*. New York: Random House, 1981.

Another well-known pollster charts a trend away from the permissive society of the sixties and seventies toward an ethic of commitment, commitment to deeper personal relationships and to spiritual and philosophical ideals. A very challenging book.

Journal Articles and Essays

Albrecht, Stan L., and Tim B. Heaton. "Secularization, Higher Education, and Religiosity." *Review of Religious Research* 26 (1984):43-58.

It is generally assumed that there is a negative relationship between education and religion. The most educated are the least religious and vice versa. This article, however, indicates that education has not necessarily had a secularizing effect on Mormons. If sustainable, this conclusion has encouraging implications for Adventist education.

Battaglia, Anthony. "Expanding the Concept of Religion: The Case of Robert N. Bellah." *Encounter* 45 (1984):171-180.

A summary analysis of Bellah's sociological work. Bellah argues that all people are religious in the sense that they find ways to come to terms with the mysteries of human existence. An "unbeliever" is simply someone who accepts the literalness of each day as the sole reality. It is Bellah's hope that Christianity can adapt to the change in modern consciousness in a way that will continue to provide motivation, meaning, and transformation for most of its adherents in years to come.

Bibby, Reginald W., and Merlin B. Brinkerhoff. "Circulation of the Saints Revisited: A Longitudinal Look at Conservative Church Growth." *Journal for the Scientific Study of Religion* 22 (1983):253-262.

Results of a survey in Canada indicate that while conservative churches are definitely growing in numbers, they are not reaching the more secular elements of society in any significant numbers.

Brooks, James A., ed. "Secularism." *Southwestern Journal of Theology* 26:2 (Spring 1984):5-86.

A collection of five essays by different authors offering a Baptist perspective on the impact of secularization on education, the media, and American politics. The final essay offers some suggestions toward a Christian response to secularism.

Cunningham, Richard B. "Christianity and Contemporary Humanism." *Review and Expositor* 81 (1984):273-289.

Distinguishes "humanism" in general from "secular humanism" in particular and articulates how Christianity should relate to the two.

Faber, Heije. "The Ministry in a Changing Society." *Perkins Journal* 34 (Fall 1980):1-27.

A superb overview of the impact secularization has had on individuals, families, churches, and religion in general. Of particular interest is the final section, which discusses the impact recent developments have had on ministers and their ministry.

Geering, Lloyd. "Secularization and Religion." In *Religious Studies in the Pacific*, 215-223. Edited by J. Hinchcliff. Auckland, N.Z.: Colloquium Publishers, 1978.

Geering sees the secularization of our age as a remarkable parallel to the developments in religion in the centuries just preceding the N.T. era. If this is correct, secularization may prove to be a divinely ordained means of preparing the world for Christ's return.

Hay, David, and Ann Morisy. "Secular Society, Religious Meanings: a Contemporary Paradox." *Review of Religious Research* 26 (1985):213-227.

A survey of religious attitudes in England. Provides useful analogies to the North American situation.

Lovelace, R. "Future Shock and Christian Hope." *Christianity Today* (5 Aug 1983), 12-16.

Brief discussion of the move from the Industrial Age into the Information Age with some religious implications.

Miller, Donald E. "Some Reflections on Secularization." *Religion in Life* 48 (1979):492-501.

The author argues that religion is not dying; it is only

taking different forms today. People still need a commitment to something greater than themselves, release from guilt, and meaningful fellowship with other human beings. Religions that meet those needs will continue to flourish in a secular age.

Stark, Rodney, and William Sims Bainbridge. "Secularization, Revival and Cult Formation." *The Annual Review of the Social Sciences of Religion* 4 (1980):85-119.

The authors argue that predictors of the triumph of secularization have mistaken conventional religious organizations for religion in general. Secularization is a self-limiting process that produces revival (sects) in the short run and innovation (cults) over the longer run. Sects are efforts by the churched to remain churched; cults are efforts by the unchurched to become churched.

________. "Secularization and Cult Formation in the Jazz Age." *Journal for the Scientific Study of Religion* 20 (1981):360-373.

The authors offer further evidence (see previous article) that secularization is a self-limiting phenomenon.

Theology is best when it is clear, without prejudice, and seasoned with the grace of Christ. Here's a book that fits the bill.

The Antichrist and the New World Order is a "plain folks" explanation of the end times for non-Adventists. Marvin Moore, author of the bestselling *Crisis of the End Time,* presents the Adventist understanding of the antichrist, America in prophecy, the close of probation, and more in clear, nonjudgmental terms. And, as with *Crisis*, our relationship to Jesus is given top priority.

Whether you have friends or loved ones who aren't Adventist, or you just want an understandable refresher course on end-time events for yourself, **The Antichrist and the New World Order** is the right book at the right time.

Priced for sharing at US$2.95/Cdn$4.00. Paper.

Available now at your local ABC, or order by phone! Call 1-800-765-6955.